The Book of
Machine Knitting

The Book of Machine Knitting

DAVID HOLBOURNE

B T BATSFORD LTD

London

© David Holbourne 1979

First published 1979

ISBN 0 7134 0542 2

Filmset in Monophoto Baskerville by
Servis Filmsetting Ltd, Manchester

Printed in Great Britain by
The Anchor Press Ltd, Tiptree, Essex
for the publishers B T Batsford Ltd
4 Fitzhardinge Street, London W1H 0AH

Contents

Acknowledgment

My thanks go to the Jones Sewing Machine Co Ltd (distributors of Brother machines), Knitmaster Ltd, The Singer Co Ltd, and Aisin (UK) Ltd (distributors of Toyota machines), for their help. They not only provided me with all the information I required, but also made machines available to me to use in the preparation of this book.

I particularly wish to thank Sue Strangway, who tested the practicality of the book by teaching herself to machine knit from it, and in the process suggested many useful improvements.

Figure 1 is reproduced by kind permission of the Science Museum London, to whom the stocking frame is lent by N. Corah & Sons Ltd Leicester. Figure 99 is reproduced by kind permission of the Post Office. Figures 97 and 99 were photographed by Bob Young.

Introduction

Beginnings of machine knitting

Machine knitting or frame knitting, as it was originally called, is much older than most people realise. The first knitting frame was built by the Reverend William Lee at Nottingham in 1589, and needed two people to operate it. According to legend, he became interested in the problem of speeding up the knitting process because whenever he called on the lady he was courting, she was too busy knitting to entertain him.

The earliest frames were narrower than today's machines as they were used exclusively for knitting stockings. Lee's first frame was quite a coarse gauge, suitable for knitting wool. He presented a pair of his woollen stockings to Queen Elizabeth in the hope of gaining her patronage. She was so disappointed that they were not silk that he went away and developed a finer frame capable of knitting silk.

When even this frame failed to gain support from the Queen for his venture, he accepted an invitation from the Marquis de Rosny to set up an industry in France. This effort came to an end with the assassination of the French king and withdrawal of official patronage. Lee died, a disappointed man, in 1610. However, after his death, stocking frame knitting became a thriving industry in both London and Nottingham.

What is machine knitting?

The fabrics produced on a knitting machine are almost identical to those produced by hand knitting. The main difference is that they are more regular, as the tension of the stitches, which in hand knitting depends on the knitter, is mechanically controlled. The simplest hand knitting is garter stitch. This is achieved by making the same basic stitch all the time. Because the work is turned round at the beginning of each new row, alternate rows are made from opposite sides of the fabric. In machine knitting the stitches are made from the same side, so the basic stitch is stocking (stockinette) stitch. Paradoxically the simple garter stitch is one of the most complicated things to do in machine knitting because it requires double ended needles that knit in opposite directions on alternate rows.

The simplest form of knitting frame, which many people learn to use as children, is a wooden cotton reel (or thread spool) with nails in it, which produces a narrow circular cord known as french knitting. The stitch is formed in the same way as in hand knitting, but instead of all the stitches in a row being collected onto the shank of one needle, each stitch is held by a separate nail. In the modern knitting machine the action of making the stitch is speeded up by the use of the latch hook, which is similar to a rug-making hook. This makes it possible to pick up the yarn for the new stitch and drop the old stitch in one smooth action.

How stitches are formed
Hand knitting
The right-hand needle is inserted into the first stitch on the left-hand needle (fig. 2a).

Figure 1 Early stocking frame (c. 1770) similar to those made by the Reverend William Lee in the sixteenth century

Figure 2a

Yarn is wrapped round the point of the right-hand needle. The right-hand needle is withdrawn from the stitch bringing a new loop of yarn with it (fig. 2b).

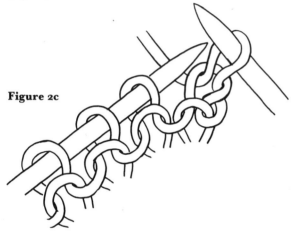

Figure 2b

The old stitch is pulled off the left-hand needle (fig. 2c).

Figure 2c

The stitch on the nail is lifted off the nail (fig. 3b).

Figure 3b

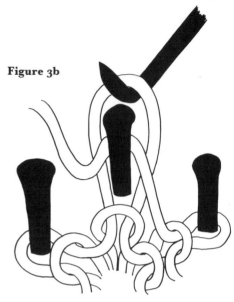

The stitch is dropped in front of the nail leaving the yarn to make a new stitch (fig. 3c).

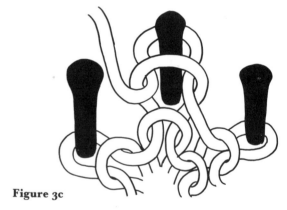

Figure 3c

French knitting
The yarn is taken round behind the nail (fig. 3a).

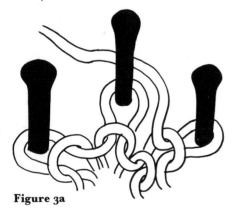

Figure 3a

Machine knitting
The stitch is held on a hook fitted with a hinged latch (fig. 4a).

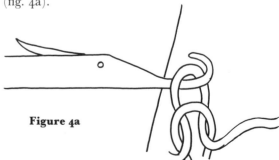

Figure 4a

The hook slides forward until the stitch is behind the latch (fig. 4b).

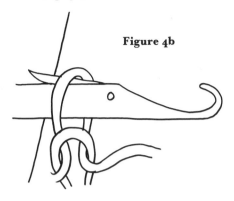

Figure 4b

The yarn is placed in the hook. The needle slides back. The stitch is pushed under the point of the latch (fig. 4c).

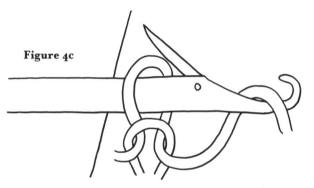

Figure 4c

As the needle moves further back, the stitch pushes the latch closed (fig. 4d).

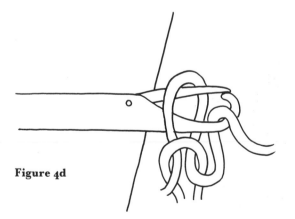

Figure 4d

As the needle returns to the starting position, the stitch slips over the closed latch. The yarn is retained within the hook to form a new stitch (fig. 4e).

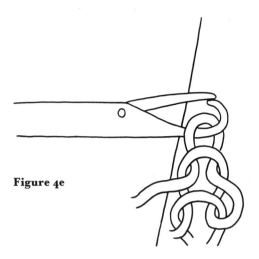

Figure 4e

The machine is required to perform two tasks for a stitch to be formed. Firstly the needle must be moved back and forth. Secondly the yarn must be fed to the hook at the right time. Both these tasks are performed by the carriage. Needles consist of two parts, the latch hook and the butt (fig. 5). They are

butt   latch hook

Figure 5

set into grooves in a metal plate called the needle bed, with the butts protruding through the grooves on top. The needle can then be moved by pushing the butt back and forth (fig. 6).

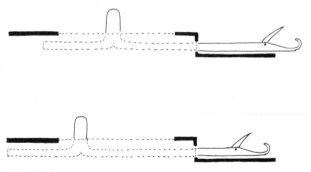

Figure 6

As the carriage is passed across the needle bed, the needle butt connects with a channel on the underside. The carriage is allowed to pass over the butt by

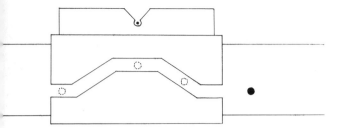

Figure 7

the needle sliding forward and back, the butt following the path of the channel (fig. 7).

The walls of the channel are made of sections called cams. They are adjustable so the butt can be made to follow varying paths to give plain, tuck or slip stitch. The yarn is held by a feeder in the centre of the sinker plate which is at the front of the carriage. It carries the yarn across the needles when they are in the forward and open position. The sinker plate also prevents the stitches moving as the needles are brought forward. The brushes on its underside push the latches open ready to take the yarn.

The structure of single knit fabrics

Figure 8 shows the loop formation of the basic single knit fabric. The technical face side is shown. Whilst it is being knitted this side is towards the machine and the knitter sees the reverse side. The term technical face is used because most knitted fabrics may be used with either side as the right side.

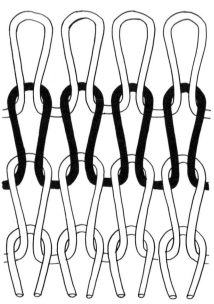

Figure 8

With some stitches the technical reverse is mostly used as the 'right' side. The black stitches form one row or course. A single vertical column of stitches is known as a wale.

The distinctive feature of a knitted fabric as compared to a woven fabric is its ability to stretch and change shape. Figure 9 shows the stitches in a knitted fabric which has been stretched lengthways. When stretched widthways it becomes more than twice as wide and less than half as long. Figure 10 shows how the loops of the stitches change shape to allow this to happen. Figure 11 shows the threads in a woven fabric. Because they run almost straight vertically and horizontally, the only stretch possible

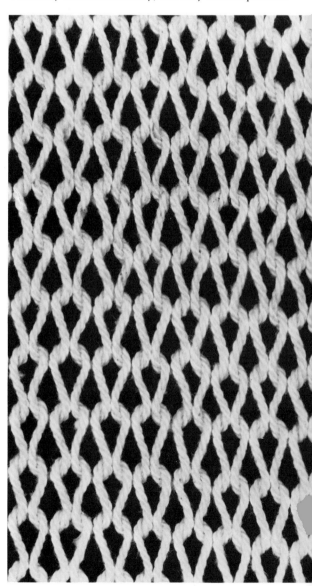

Figure 9

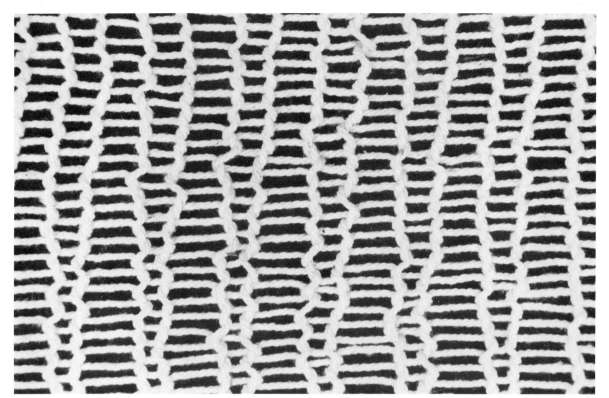

Figure 10

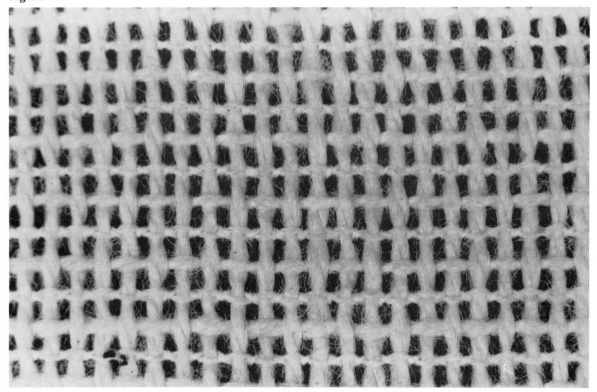

Figure 11

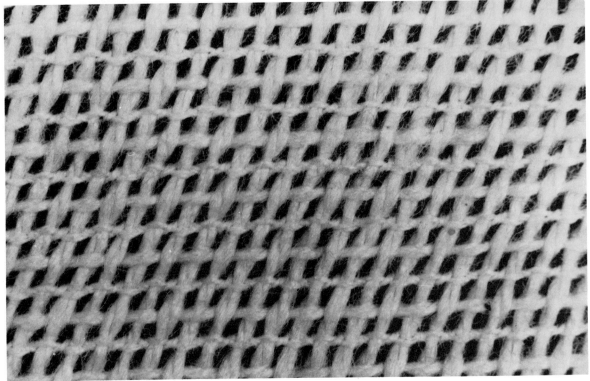

Figure 12

is diagonally, and this is only slight (fig. 12). However the overall proportions of the fabric remain the same.

Although there are many different patterns and effects possible in single knitting, they are all based on one or a combination of the following four variations of the basic stocking (stockinette) stitch.

Slip stitch

A slip stitch is formed by one or more needles remaining inactive as the row is knitted. This produces a float on the surface of the fabric (fig. 13). Slip stitch is an example of a stitch where the pattern shows on the technical reverse side. It is also the basis of two colour or fairisle patterning (fig. 14).

This pattern example of alternate stitches in black and white is achieved as follows. One row is knitted in white, slipping odd stitches. One row is knitted in black, slipping even stitches. On the stitches that were slipped on the white row no white stitch shows on the face side. These stitches were knitted on the black row, so a black stitch shows their place. On more sophisticated machines the white and black rows are knitted in one movement of the carriage, the white slightly ahead of the black. Fairisle is an example of a stitch where the pattern shows on the face side.

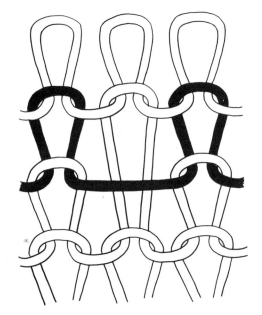

Figure 13

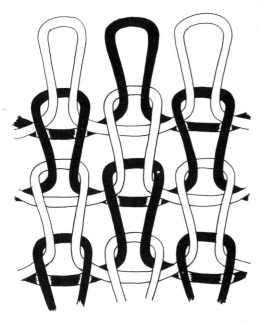

Figure 14

Tuck stitch

A tuck stitch (fig. 15) is formed when a needle moves out far enough to collect the new yarn but not far enough for the old stitch to slip behind the latch, so that when the needle returns to its starting position it retains both the old stitch and the new yarn (fig. 16). This stitch has many uses for effects on both the face and reverse sides of the fabric.

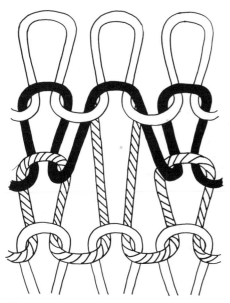

Figure 15

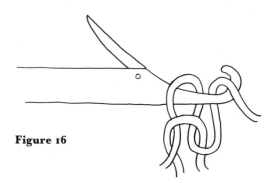

Figure 16

Lace stitch

Lace stitch (fig. 17) is also referred to as stitch transfer, and this describes very well how it is achieved. A stitch is transferred from its needle to the next needle and the knitting is continued. The empty needle picks up the new yarn and continues to knit, leaving a hole where the transfer was made.

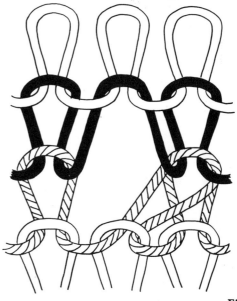

Figure 17

Inlay

Inlay is also referred to as weaving. It is not strictly a stitch variation. Stocking stitch is made in the normal way but an extra yarn is taken across the needle bed first, passing under and over alternate needles. Then, when the row is knitted, the inlay yarn is caught under alternate stitches (fig. 18). Because the inlay yarn passes across the fabric without making loops, it prevents the fabric from being stretched widthways. This lateral stability in inlay fabrics sets it apart from other knitted fabrics, and must be taken into consideration when deciding how to use it.

15

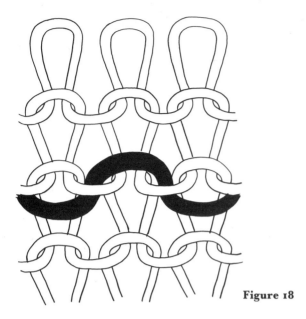

Figure 18

Types of machine

Machines can be divided into two main categories: those with one set of needles all working in the same direction (fig. 19), and those with two sets of needles set opposite each other (fig. 20). The first type produces a basic single fabric in stocking stitch and is known as a single bed machine. The second produces a double knit or rib fabric and is known as a double bed or 'V' bed machine. The vast majority of domestic machines are single beds. Most manufacturers also supply an extra bed, often called a ribber or ribbing attachment, which can be attached to the main machine to convert it from single to double bed.

All the stitches and techniques described in this book may be done on the basic single bed machine. Most beginners find it easier to learn on a single bed machine, partly because it is simpler and partly because it is easier to see what is going on. The visibility of the knitting also makes is easier to improvise and develop new patterns on the machine. Once mastered, they offer scope for infinite invention and variation. The ribbing attachment is useful for knitting ribbed edgings, but there are alternative methods possible on the single bed. For extensive work in rib, a true double bed machine is preferable.

There are industrial machines which are hand powered, and they are usually 'V' beds, but most industrial machines are powered by electric motors. Power units are available for some domestic machines and are designed to convert them to industrial use. The fastest industrial machines have circular needle beds. They are particularly efficient for two reasons. Firstly, the knitting action is continuous; there is no need to stop and change direction at the end of each row. Secondly, it is possible to start knitting a second row before the first one has finished. These machines often have up to 64 staggered rows knitting at once.

Figure 19

16

Figure 20

Which Machine?

Most home knitting machines are of similar design: single bed models with 200 needles. They are 6 gauge, giving a knitting width of 89cm ($35\frac{1}{2}$ inches). Gauge denotes the number of needles per inch (this traditional method is used universally, even in metric countries), but the size of the stitch is adjustable. Because of this, and depending on the type of stitch and thickness of yarn, the number of stitches per inch when the fabric comes off the machine may vary from 5 to 8, giving maximum knitting widths from approximately 92 to 60cm (37 to 24 inches).

Note that the widest knitting possible is greater than the width of the needle bed. This is mainly in tuck stitch where the stitches push outwards as they come off the machine. Ribbing attachments are available for most makes. Most of these machines are made in Japan, though often marketed by British or American companies. For example, the Japanese-manufactured Silver machine is sold as Knitmaster in England, Studio in the United States, Empisal in Europe and Singer in Mexico and Canada. Similarly, the Juki machine is sold under the name of Singer in England and Juki in the United States. The Toyota and Brother machines are sold under their own brand names throughout most countries of the world.

There are three exceptions to this basic specification. They are the Knitmaster 250, the Passap Duomatic and the Superba. The Knitmaster 250 is similar except that it is a 5 gauge machine. The Duomatic, which is Swiss made, and the Superba are the only true double bed machines for home use.

There are two significant ways in which the main group of machines varies. The first is in the way pattern needles are selected, i.e. how, in each row, one can control which stitches will be plain and which will be fancy. The second is in the size of the pattern repeat. This affects both the size and variety of patterns available.

On the simplest machines, pattern needles are selected by bringing them forward, either by hand or with a needle pusher (fig. 21), at the beginning of each row. Needle pushers are available in simple sequences such as 1×1, 1×3, 2×2, etc. These would give, respectively, a pattern stitch every other stitch, a pattern stitch every fourth stitch, and alternate pairs of pattern and plain stitches. Although selecting needles by hand is slow, it has the advantage that there is no set repeat size and the pattern could be non-repeating across the whole width of the knitting.

More efficient ways of selecting pattern needles are provided by a detachable selector or by lever. With the selector one repeat is selected by hand. The selector is then passed across the needle bed and repeats the sequence across the whole width of the knitting. With the lever system, one repeat is selected by pressing a set of buttons. A lever is then operated which brings needles forward in that sequence across the whole width of the knitting. In both cases this operation has to be repeated each time a pattern row is knitted.

On all the newer models pattern stitches are selected by the Jacquard or punch card system. Each row of the pattern is punched out in holes and blank spaces on a plastic sheet. Once the card is fed into the machine and the type of stitch has been selected, the knitter only has to pass the carriage back and forth as for plain knitting. The sequence of holes and blank spaces on the first row of the card controls which stitches will be plain and which will be pattern stitches across the whole width of the knitting. The card then moves down one row automatically ready for the next row of knitting. The way the pattern is conveyed from the card to the needle varies from model to model. Most punch card machines have a maximum pattern repeat of 24 stitches, compared with maximum repeats of 8 to 12 stitches on the selector and lever models. Superba has a pattern repeat of over 24 stitches, and one Knitmaster model has a pattern repeat of 64 stitches.

The main advantage of a punch card machine is that it will knit patterned fabrics as quickly as plain ones and with less risk of making a mistake in the pattern. It is also capable of knitting pattern repeats up to 10cm (4 inches) wide, whereas the simpler machines have a maximum repeat of about 5cm (2 inches).

Its disadvantages are that it is more expensive, it is physically harder to work because the sophisticated mechanisms make the carriage heavy, and its dependence on punch cards makes it rather inflexible when it comes to trying out new ideas. It is designed to knit tuck, slip, two colour fairisle, inlay, and either true or imitation lace, and it will knit these quickly, but only in patterns based on the cards available. If you do not have an appropriate card, you have to buy one or punch a new one yourself. This is rather time consuming if you only want to try an idea to see what it looks like.

There are other types of patterning besides the basic ones which punch card machines are designed to do, which involve a certain amount of hand patterning or the use of more than two colours at once, and for these a simpler machine is more suitable.

The Toyota 787 combines the advantages of both types of machine, having both punch card and button systems of needle selection. On the Brother, Singer and Juki models it is possible to select needles by hand. On the Knitmaster and Studio machines no alternative to punch card selection is available.

To sum up: punch card machines are best for speed of production, simpler machines are best for flexibility in designing and for price.

Non punch card models

The Brother machine differs from the rest of the group in several respects. In its favour are the facts that its lever needle selection is appreciably faster than either mechanical selector or manual selection, and that it comes equipped with a lace carriage. Without this attachment it is not practicable to do lace stitch over large areas, although it is possible to do this manually, and the stitch may be used in small amounts such as in borders. Until recently a weak point on the Brother machine was its tensioning system. It did not allow independent tensioning of the two yarns. Also threading was slightly more complicated, and the springs were positioned in such a way that they sometimes caught on each other and obstructed progress. These faults have been rectified on some of the newer models.

Although, as can be seen, these machines are quite similar, the price range is quite wide in the UK. In the USA, comparable models are sold at the same price.

MODEL	NEEDLE SELECTION	MAXIMUM REPEAT
Brother KH 588	lever	8 stitches
Knitmaster/Studio 250	selector	12 stitches
Knitmaster/Studio 310	selector	12 stitches
Passap F200	hand	—
Toyota K 510	hand (selector available as optional extra)	10 stitches

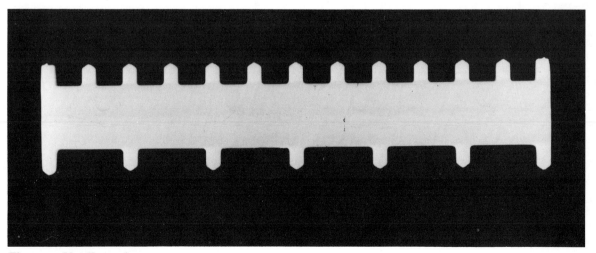

Figure 21 Needle pusher

MODEL	LACE CARRIAGE	ALTERNATIVE PATTERNING	EXTRA PATTERNING FACILITIES	ACCESSORIES INCLUDED
Brother KH 830	yes	manual	knits alternate rows in contrasting stitches	—
Knitmaster/Studio 323/326	no	no	attachments for ease of partial patterning	built in knit radar optional
Singer/Juki Memomatic	yes	manual	knits alternate rows in contrasting stitches	ball winder and card punch
Toyota 787	yes	buttons	automatic single motif	—

Punch card models

Knitmaster and Studio models are the highest priced machines, including optional built-in knit radar, and a complete set of basic garment patterns. The convenience and ease of use of the Knitmaster knit radar makes this machine the best for making a wide variety of garment shapes. Its main disadvantage is that it is impossible to select pattern needles manually. It will not knit true stitch transfer lace, although the Knitmaster imitation lace is quicker to do and gives a similar effect.

The Brother machines are well made and efficient machines, and have the lightest carriage which makes them less tiring to use. The unique self-selecting lace carriage makes complicated lace patterns quick to do. Their one minor disadvantage is the design of the yarn take up spring, which tends to get in the way of the knitter, and to become tangled when more than one yarn is being used.

The Toyota machine is the most versatile machine with its choice of punch card, button, or manual needle selection plus a very simple to operate single motif control. The Toyota uses the same bed as the Brother and Knitmaster machines.

Singer and Juki machines are in the lower price bracket. They are particularly heavy to operate because the pattern mechanism is mounted in the carriage. A ribber is available for some of them but details such as the clamps and the tensioner do not work as well as they should.

Shaping aids

The terms knit radar, knit leader and knit tracer all refer to the same type of device. It is an attachment which makes it possible to draw out the shape required and then commence knitting, without working out the sequence of increases and decreases first. The drawing is fed onto a roller. On the front of the roller is a gauge which indicates the number of stitches required for the width shown on the drawing. As each row is knitted, the drawing automatically moves down the equivalent of one row too. So at the end of each row the gauge indicates how many stitches should be on the needles, and tells you whether to increase or decrease.

The stitch gauge and the amount the drawing moves down each row can be adjusted according to the fineness or coarseness of the knitting. Shaping aids may be fitted to punch card and non punch card machines. If you want to be able to design varied shapes of garment quickly and easily, a simple machine with a shaping aid is a better investment than a punch card machine without one.

Knitmaster and Studio knit radar differs from Toyota and Brother models in several respects. The latter work from full-scale patterns which are drawn out onto a special plastic sheet. The Knitmaster model works from half-scale patterns which are drawn out on paper, and is sold with a set of basic patterns in all adult and children's sizes. There are advantages and disadvantages to both types. The full-scale pattern is simpler to draw out and involves fewer calculations, and as the plastic sheet is transparent it is possible to trace direct from dressmaking patterns. On the other hand, a full-scale tracer takes up more space both in use and when stored. Moreover, because the pattern must be traced onto the plastic sheet provided, each time a new pattern is required the previous pattern must be washed off and the new one traced out. The Knitmaster knit radar is compact, and the patterns provided, as well as your own patterns if you wish to make them, can be filed away for future use. On the other hand there is more calculation required to scale down patterns to half size, and this may lead to confusion.

After sales service

Each machine comes with a manual explaining its operation. The Brother book has large clear illustrations, but covers only basic techniques. Knitmaster and Studio offer three books: a manual, a stitch pattern book, and instructions for making basic garments. The information in them is comprehensive, but rather too compressed and not always clear. It is more suitable for an experienced knitter changing to a newer machine than for a complete beginner. Singer and Juki offer three similar books which are less comprehensive but more clearly laid out. Toyota's manual strikes a good balance between comprehensiveness and clarity.

Regardless of where a Knitmaster machine is purchased, the company offers 5 one-hour lessons at home from one of their own tutors. Singer knitting machines are available only from selected Singer sewing machine shops. The dealers offer 3 one-hour lessons which are given in the shop. Because the shop conducts the lessons during business hours, the lessons may be interrupted, and it may be difficult to concentrate. However the tutor attached to the shop is always available to answer queries and give advice at any time. Purchasers of Brother machines have a choice of a postal course or lessons from the dealer. Toyota machines are available only from specialist knitting machine dealers, and tuition is at the discretion of the dealer. Studio dealers have the option of offering lessons, and most do.

Help and advice may be needed after the initial tuition period. Besides the tutor in the shop, Singer employs a national knitting adviser who may be reached direct by telephone during office hours. Owners of Knitmaster machines may make an appointment for extra tuition or specialised advice at Knitmaster's London school. Studio dealers offer lessons for all levels as well as seminars for the advanced knitter. Purchasers of Brother and Toyota machines must depend on their local dealer for advice.

Knitmaster and Studio offer the widest selection of stitch and garment patterns, as well as publishing a magazine with patterns. Brother publishes several very comprehensive books of stitch patterns as well as a magazine. Both Singer and Toyota publish books of basic garment patterns plus occasional individual patterns. Many garment patterns and all punch card patterns are interchangeable from one machine to another in the newer models.

The companies vary slightly in the maintenance and repair services offered. Knitmaster and Studio machines may be returned direct to the company or to a dealer who will have been company trained. Toyota models must be returned to the dealer who will have been advised by Toyota on the repair of their machines. Singer and Juki machines are returned to a central maintenance department via a shop. Owners of Brother machines in the UK must contact the Jones Sewing Machine Company who will arrange for a local maintenance engineer to call. Owners in the USA should contact their dealer.

Second-hand machines

Second-hand machines may be purchased from dealers or through private advertisements. Many are virtually unused because the owners never learnt to use them properly.

Dealers' second-hand machines have usually been traded in for more recent models by knitters. They are normally thoroughly overhauled before resale. If the various stitches are tried out on the machine before purchase and it performs them with no difficulty, it is unlikely that the machine will have any faults that might show up later. If the machine has not been used for some time it will be stiff and heavy, but will improve with regular use.

The main drawback in buying a second-hand machine is the lack of initial tuition and advice, although normally a dealer will at least briefly demonstrate the use of the machine at the time of purchase.

Yarns

Care in choosing yarn is the most important factor in deciding the quality and suitability of a knitted fabric, as well as being a major element in its design. Quality in a fabric encompasses such things as handle, drape, whether it will hold its shape in wash and wear, and whether it provides the insulation or ventilation required for a particular use.

Design in relation to knitting is usually thought of in terms of pattern, particularly colour pattern. But just as important are factors such as texture, structure, opacity and sheen. Even colour quality depends on the type of fibre to which the dye pigment has been applied, and whether the yarn is such that it absorbs or reflects light. Lack of care and variety in choosing yarn is the main reason why so much home knitting lacks style, in spite of the complexity and variety of patterns possible on modern machines.

Increasing the choice of yarn and including fancy and effect yarns does not necessarily increase the cost greatly, especially if use is made of wholesale suppliers, and other sources of yarn not normally associated with home knitting. To make the best of the wide range of yarns available, a basic knowledge of the various types of fibre and yarn and their qualities is necessary.

Fibres

The raw material from which yarns are made is called fibre. It comes in two forms, staple and filament. Staple fibre is made of lots of separate pieces, their length depending on the source of the fibre. To make yarn these fibres are joined together by twisting them together or spinning them. In this way their length may be extended indefinitely. Filament comes in a continuous length, long enough to be used as a yarn without any further processing.

Both staple and filament fibres may be natural or man-made. Natural fibres are either animal or vegetable. Wool from sheep is the most common animal fibre. Fibre from the coats of other animals is called hair to distinguish it from sheep's wool. The ones of most interest to knitters are mohair, angora and cashmere. Mohair is the hair of the angora goat. Angora is the hair of the angora rabbit. Cashmere is the hair of the cashmere goat.

Cotton is the most common vegetable fibre. It is the packing around the seeds in the seed pod of the cotton plant. Linen is also a vegetable fibre. It comes from the inner layers of the stalk of the flax plant. Linen is not particularly suitable for knitting as it lacks the necessary elasticity. All the natural fibres mentioned so far are staple fibres. The only natural fibre of the filament type is silk, which is made by the silk worm. It is extruded in a similar way to the way in which a spider makes the thread for its web; however, the silk worm produces a double filament, and for a different purpose. The silk worm is actually a type of caterpillar, and uses the silk to make a cocoon before beginning its transformation into a moth.

Man-made fibres are all produced in filament form. They are made by squeezing a liquid through very fine holes in a similar way to toothpaste being squeezed from a tube. Then when the liquid is in this long filament form it is set into shape. Sometimes the liquid is molten and sets as it cools. Sometimes it sets through evaporation as it is exposed to the air. With other types of fibre the setting is achieved by dipping the filaments into a chemical. The main raw materials for man-made fibres are wood, coal and oil. Once the filament is made it is often chopped up into staple and then spun.

Man-made fibres can be divided into regenerated fibres and synthetic fibres. Those using wood as the raw material are of the regenerated variety. The basic substance of wood is cellulose and this material is used to make viscose and acetate rayon.

Fibres made from coal and oil are synthetic. The raw material is transformed into a substance with a completely new molecular structure of a fibrous nature. The main synthetic fibres are nylon, polyester, and acrylic.

Wool

Wool is a most important fibre for the knitter for several reasons. It has unique insulating properties due to its natural kinkyness, which allows air to be trapped between the individual fibres. It also recovers its shape well after stretching or distortion and does not bag permanently, due to this same characteristic. The fibres act as tiny springs which stretch when the fabric is stretched and spring back to their natural shape when the fabric is relaxed. Wool absorbs moisture well, which is an advantage for some types of clothing. It is resistant to burning. Although it is very resilient it is only moderately hard wearing. It does require care in handling and particularly when washing.

Besides the natural kink, its other marked characteristic is the scaliness of the fibres. These scales are too small to be seen by the naked eye but they have an important effect on the behaviour of woollen fabrics. They act as barbs so that when the fibres are rubbed together they can only move in one direction and cannot return to their original position. This is the cause of both the felting and the shrinking to which wool is prone. Heat, moisture and movement all encourage this tendency, and this is why care in washing is so important.

The main things to remember are: use warm, not hot, water for both washing and rinsing, squeeze excess water out gently, do not wring, and dry flat, making sure the garment is in its correct shape as it dries. If cold water is used for rinsing, the natural softness will be impaired, and because wool is sensitive to chemicals, only soap flakes or powder should be used, never detergent. Iron gently with a warm iron.

Recently a type of wool has been developed which will stand the rigours of machine washing without felting. This has been achieved by chlorination, which removes the tips of the scales, and then by a fine resin coating. The fibres are then able to move against each other in either direction.

Wool fibre may be used to make woollen or worsted yarns. Woollen yarns are made from shorter staple wool. The wool is carded before it is spun. In the carding process the fibre is teased between wire brushes to remove impurities and to separate out all the individual fibres. Woollen yarns are light and bulky.

Worsted yarns are made from longer staple fibres which are passed through an extra process called combing before being spun. After the carding process the fibres are separate and lie at random to one another. The combing process makes the fibres more or less parallel, and this, combined with the extra length, produces smoother, stronger, more lustrous yarns.

Woollen yarn has better insulating properties, is softer and uses less weight to knit a given area. Because worsted yarns are stronger they may be spun more finely, and they are more hard wearing. The difference between the two is easily seen by comparing a shetland yarn, which is woollen, with a good quality 4 ply fingering wool, which is worsted. They are about the same thickness, but in every ounce of shetland there is approximately 50% more length.

Merino sheep are bred only for their wool, not for both wool and meat as other breeds. Merino is the shortest, finest, and most kinky type of wool. It is the warmest and most comfortable next to the skin, but not the most hard wearing. Botany wool is merino which comes from Botany Bay.

Because wool is such a resilient fibre it is possible to reprocess woollen fabrics by shredding them and using the fibre to spin new yarns. Pure new wool is a term which may only be applied to wool which does not contain any reprocessed fibre. This term and the International Wool Secretariat's Woolmark are designed to avoid any misunderstanding on this point. The term 'all wool' may be applied to woollen products which are a blend of new and reprocessed fibre. Shoddy is the term applied to fibre obtained by shredding soft woollen rags.

Woollen yarns, particularly shetland and tweed types, are often spun in oil. They are soft yarns which lack strength. The added oil gives them the necessary strength to make it possible to knit them without breaking. Once the fabric has been knitted, the oil is washed out, making them soft and warm. They may be deliberately agitated during the first washing to felt them slightly. When deciding at what tension to knit these yarns, it is important to allow for the bulking up that occurs during washing, or you may end up with something too heavy and stiff.

Hair

The animal hairs are much more expensive than wool, which is why they are usually used in blends with wool. Mohair and angora are longer, more lustrous fibres than wool. Their long fibres may be teased out at the yarn or fabric stage to give a hairy surface effect. Because they are so long, this pile may be raised without weakening or disintegrating the yarn. Cashmere is a very soft fibre with a natural lustre and is often used in its natural fawn colour. Alpaca, vicuna, and camel also come in this category, but are not of interest to the knitter.

Cotton

In contrast to wool, cotton lacks elasticity and is smooth and cool to the touch. Its lack of elasticity makes it less easy to knit and more liable to break or snag. It lacks the resilience of wool, which makes it prone to creasing and bagging. It is also highly inflammable, which makes it unsuitable for articles such as children's nightwear, although fire-retarding treatments can be applied. It is strong and hard wearing and may be spun very fine. It is not sensitive to heat or chemicals, and may therefore be washed in hot water with detergents and bleach, and may be hot ironed.

It is also highly absorbent. Cotton fibres and yarns do not shrink, but cotton fabrics may shrink. This is due to the fibres absorbing moisture and swelling up, so that more length of yarn is taken up as one loop passes over another. This is not, however, a great problem in loosely constructed materials like knitted fabrics.

The best and strongest cotton yarns are made from the longest staple fibre which is Sea Island or Egyptian cotton. They are used for the finest yarns and are not particularly relevant to the home knitter. American cotton is of medium staple length and strength, and Indian is the shortest and poorest quality. Mercerised cotton is particularly suitable for knitting because it is stronger and smoother than untreated cotton, and this compensates to some extent for its lack of elasticity, and reduces the risk of yarn breakages. In the mercerising process the cotton is treated with caustic soda which causes the flat fibres to swell and become round. This gives a permanent lustrous finish.

Silk

Silk combines great strength with softness and, because it is a filament yarn, high lustre too. It has good elasticity and resilience, which makes it retain its shape well and resist creasing. However, like wool, it requires delicate washing and ironing. Most silk comes from cultivated worms fed on mulberry leaves. Wild silk comes from Tussah silk worms which feed mainly on oak leaves. Tussah silk is coarse and irregular and lacks the lustre and softness of cultivated silk. Ends and waste lengths of filament are used to make spun silk, which is resilient and elastic but less lustrous.

Viscose Rayon

Rayon was the first man-made fibre, and was developed as a substitute for silk. Viscose rayon used to be called art silk or artificial silk, and was used as filament. It is now often cut up into staple and spun, which produces a yarn similar to cotton in appearance but with more lustre. It is also similar to cotton in that it is highly flammable, and creases and bags even more than cotton. It loses strength when wet, so care must be taken when washing. It is very absorbent and swells as it absorbs moisture, causing the same sort of shrinking as occurs with cotton. It melts if a hot iron is brought into contact with it. However, it is relatively cheap, and its high lustre makes it a decorative fibre.

Acetate rayon

Acetate is also made of cellulose. It has better qualities of crease resistance and resilience. It is less absorbent than viscose and therefore less liable to shrinkage, but it is inflammable and also melts as it burns. It is extremely sensitive to heat and only a moderately warm iron may be used on it. Dicel, Celanese and Celafibre are trade names.

Triacetate

Sold under the trade names Tricel and Arnel, it is similar to acetate but does not melt so easily and may be heat set to make it drip dry. This means that it does not absorb much moisture, and will dry quickly after washing and be relatively crease free.

Nylon

Nylon was the first synthetic fibre to be developed. It is much stronger and harder wearing than any of the fibres mentioned so far. It hardly absorbs moisture at all which makes it very quick drying, and it is resistant to shrinking, creasing and bagging. However, it has an unpleasant feel, is translucent, and the lack of absorption and ventilation makes it uncomfortable to wear next to the skin. It is often used blended with wool in knitting yarns. The nylon gives strength and durability, and the wool gives warmth and softness. Because it melts at high temperatures it is not particularly a fire hazard. Bri-nylon, Celon, Liana and Cantrece are trade names for nylon.

Polyester

Polyester is called Terylene (UK) and Dacron (USA). Trevira, Tergal, Fortrel and Kodel are also trade names for this fibre. It is very similar to nylon in its strength, durability and drip-dry qualities, but it has a more sympathetic, less synthetic feel. It is also often used blended with wool, but because of its more natural handle, a greater proportion of the blend may be synthetic than is the case with nylon, without spoiling the feel. Because it is less elastic than nylon, it is less suitable for knitting yarn.

Acrylic

Orlon, Acrilan and Courtelle are all trade names for acrylic fibre. It is not as strong and hard wearing as nylon or polyester, but it is much closer in feel to wool, although limper, and therefore is more often used on its own. Although it has a low absorbency, it stretches easily when damp, and so requires very careful washing and ironing if it is not to become limp and shapeless. It should not be steam ironed. Only a barely warm, dry iron should be used.

Types of yarn

Yarn from filament may be monofilament or multi-filament. Monofilament means one single strand of relatively thick fibre being used on its own. Multi-filament yarns are groups of filaments either lying parallel or twisted together.

Staple fibre must be spun to make a yarn. It is drawn out and twisted at the same time in several stages until the degree of fineness required has been reached. The intermediate stage is called roving. If it is twisted lightly it will give a bulky, soft yarn with good insulating properties but little strength. If it is twisted tightly it will be hard and strong. It may be twisted clockwise or anti-clockwise and is known as 'S' twist or 'Z' twist yarn according to whether the direction of twist corresponds to the diagonal of an 's' or a 'z'.

The yarn that is produced by spinning is called singles yarn. Often these singles yarns are doubled or plied together to make thicker yarn. Doubled yarn is known as 2 ply, 3 ply, etc., according to the number of singles ends that have been combined. The term twofold means the same thing. They are usually twisted together in the opposite direction to the twist of the original singles yarn, so that if the singles ends are 'Z' twist the doubled yarn will be 'S' twist. This gives a balanced yarn which is less likely to curl and knot up. Unbalanced yarns also have a tendency to distort the knitted fabric so that it grows diagonally.

Filament and staple spun yarns are sometimes doubled together for special effects. Several doubled yarns may be twisted together to produce a yarn with a cable effect. In hand knitting the terms 2 ply, 3 ply and 4 ply are generally accepted as referring to yarns of a specific weight or thickness. Outside the range of hand knitting yarns the ply does not give an indication of the thickness of a yarn because it does not specify the weight of the original singles yarns. In the production of hand knitting yarns a standard weight of singles yarn is mostly used.

Fancy yarns

Fancy effects in yarns may be achieved with colour or texture, and may be added at the fibre, spinning or doubling stage. When different colours are mixed at the fibre stage it is called a blend. It gives a soft, subtle effect. 'Heather Mixture' refers to this type of yarn and shetland yarns are often blends. A marl is a twofold yarn in which each end is spun from roving of two contrasting colours. It gives a more definite mottled effect than blending. A mixture yarn is one in which two or more ends of contrasting colour have been doubled. All these multi-coloured yarns may be called tweed yarns. Yarns may be dyed or printed in sections of contrasting colour. 'Rainbow' yarns are of this type.

Texture may be added to synthetic fibres because of their thermoplastic quality. This means that if they are crimped or curled and then heated to the right temperature they will remain permanently in this shape. The principle is the same as setting hair with curlers except that the set is permanent. Helanca and Ban-lon are both textured forms of filament nylon. The term high bulk refers to textured forms of synthetic staple fibres. The texturing process is intended to give synthetic fibres the same desirable properties which wool has due to its natural kink.

An example of a texture effect which is introduced at the spinning stage is seen in slub yarns. They are spun deliberately unevenly with sections of tightly twisted yarn alternating with sections of soft fibre which is hardly twisted at all. This type of yarn is commonly spun from wool, cotton and viscose rayon. It may be used as a singles yarn or doubled with a regular yarn. It is difficult to obtain satis-factory results in knitting with this type of yarn, particularly in the singles form. This is because if a tension loose enough to knit the thickest parts is chosen, the areas of thin yarn will be knitted too loosely. Doubled yarns or two ends of singles knitted together is more satisfactory as the thin and thick parts even themselves out. Coarse slub yarns may only be used as laying-in yarn with a regular yarn knitting.

A slub yarn may be doubled with a straight yarn. When a fine straight yarn is doubled with a bulky textured yarn it is known as a binder as it gives most

Figure 22 Fancy yarns: (left to right) loop, gimp, bouclé, slub, chenille

of the strength of the finished yarn. The fine yarn tends to be fairly straight, and the fancy yarn spirals round it. Roving is doubled with a finer yarn in this way and is known as spiral twist. Another example of a spun effect is nep. This has intermittent spots of fibre of contrasting colour caught into it. It is this method which gives donegal tweed its characteristic appearance.

The next group of fancy effects are achieved at the doubling stage, and depend on feeding the ends being doubled at different speeds or at changing speeds, which causes the yarn which has been fed in fastest to loop or snarl up. Loop yarns have two binder yarns twisted tightly and one bulky yarn fed in more rapidly so that it forms definite loops. Mohair is often used for loop yarn because the fibres

are long enough to make large loops. Loop yarns are sometimes referred to as poodle yarns.

Bouclé means ringlet, and it describes a yarn of the same type although often the loops are so small that they appear merely as bumps on the surface of the yarn. Gimp and snarl yarns are similar but they usually have only one binder yarn, and the thicker yarn snarls up into a tight hard bump instead of curling out. Only the finer qualities of these fancy doubled yarns are suitable for machine knitting in the normal way because the loops and snarls tend to catch on needles and feeders.

Brushed yarns are usually made at least partly from long-haired angora or mohair. The yarn is spun in the normal way and then the long hairs are teased out with wire brushes to give a soft furry effect. Brushed yarns must be heavily waxed to smooth down the hairs before they can be knitted. The surface is then brushed up again after knitting.

They can more easily be used as laying-in yarn.

Chenille is produced in a very different way from all the other fancy yarns. First a fabric is woven with fine strong yarns in one direction and soft bulky yarns in the other. The fine yarns are twisted round each other in pairs as they are woven in what is called a leno weave. The fabric is then cut up into tiny strips only two threads wide, in the direction of the fine yarns. The resulting fringe of the thicker yarn is what gives it the distinctive chenille appearance. Chenille is usually made of cotton although viscose and cotton/viscose blends are also used. Only the pure cotton variety has the true soft chenille feel. All but the finest weights are difficult to knit with. The strength of the yarn is entirely in the binder and its bulk is out of proportion to its strength, so it breaks very easily. As with all highly textured yarns it may be used for laying in without any problems.

Metallic yarns, of which Lurex is the best known brand, are made of thin strips of aluminium which is covered with a plastic film. The film may be clear or gold or of any other translucent colour. This thin strip is sometimes used on its own, but is very fine and slippery and hard to control because it breaks and tangles easily. More often, it is doubled with rayon to make an all-over shiny yarn, or with wool, to give an intermittent glitter effect. It is used purely for its decorative visual qualities as it imparts a harsh unsympathetic handle if too much is used in proportion to other fibres.

Choice of yarn

The main restriction on types of yarn chosen is their thickness in relation to the size of the needle hook and the gauge of the machine. With a normal 6 gauge machine the upper limit set by the gauge is 4 ply fingering or its equivalent. However, by knitting on selected needles, for example using only every other needle, or two out of every three, the gauge may be effectively reduced. It is therefore possible to knit thicker yarns, but only up to a size which will fit into the needle hook easily. It is possible to incorporate even thicker yarns into a design by laying in whilst knitting with a thinner yarn.

There is no practical limit to how thin a yarn may be knitted, although with very fine yarns the springs of the yarn tensioner fail to grip properly and it becomes difficult to maintain the constantly controlled feeding of the yarn to the needle, which is necessary for efficient knitting. There is a limit to how small a stitch may be made. This is determined by the size of the closed latch hook over which each stitch must pass. With a very fine yarn the fabric will be so open and unstable as to be of little use, although tucking or combining with thicker yarns in a pattern will overcome this.

There are several ways of making use of yarns which in the normal way would be too fine. The simplest method is to feed several single yarns into the machine as if they were one. Knitting three ends together does not give the same effect as knitting a yarn made by twisting those three ends together, because in the former case the yarns run parallel and in the latter they are twisted round each other. The fabric knitted from the three separate ends is thinner, has less bounce, and a harsher handle than the one knitted with an equivalent 3 ply yarn.

There are, for some purposes, better ways of making use of a thin yarn which on its own makes a fabric too flimsy to use. By knitting alternate stitches all over in either slip or tuck, the amount of yarn required to knit one finished row is increased by at least 50%, giving a bulkier and more opaque fabric. Although the reverse side will show an all-over slip or tuck pattern, the face side will still have the appearance of a plain fabric. If the machine being used will knit fairisle as quickly as it knits slip or tuck, then this stitch may be used in the same way. Fairisle is knitted in the normal way in a bird's eye pattern. Instead of using contrasting colours however, the same yarn is used in both feeders, so that the face side appears to be a plain fabric. This is a good way of avoiding the harshness associated with knitting several ends together, as fairisle always gives a softer, bouncier fabric than plain knitting. All these methods may be used with one or more ends in the feeder, depending on the thickness of the yarn.

The other restriction on the choice of yarn, often combined with extreme thickness, is on extreme or exaggerated texture. Highly textured and bulky yarns are often difficult and sometimes impossible to knit, because the bumps, loops, or long hairs catch and tangle on the yarn tensioner, on the feeders, and on the needles themselves. The problem of catching on the tensioner may be overcome by placing the ball of yarn on the floor in front of the machine, and feeding the yarn straight into the sinker plate feed, with it running over the left hand, and using the thumb to control the tension. Catching on needles may be avoided by using only alternate needles to knit, by knitting with a plain yarn and laying in the textured yarn, or by a combination of both methods. Repeated waxing before knitting helps enormously with these yarns.

Very shiny or slippery yarns present the same

Figure 23 Fabric growing diagonally

problems of tensioning as fine yarns. They can be overcome to some extent by winding the yarn twice round the disk spring. There is an added problem with slippery yarns that once the end of the yarn is pulled, several layers of yarn slip off the cone at once and become tangled. This problem is avoided by taking the toe of an old stocking, tying it tightly over the cone, and feeding the yarn end through a small hole cut in the top. The stocking, if tied tightly enough, then holds the bulk of the yarn in place whilst allowing the end of yarn to pull through the hole. Never attempt to rewind slippery yarns into balls as they will not remain firmly wound in this form, but will unwind and tangle even whilst being stored.

Other yarns, particularly some designed as weaving yarns, also present problems for the machine knitter. They include highly twisted yarns

which curl and snag in the feeders, and singles yarns which have a directional bias, so that, as stitches are formed, they pull to one side instead of forming a symmetrical loop. The fabric therefore grows diagonally instead of at right angles, and accurate shaping is impossible (fig. 23). Yarns with little or no elasticity present problems. Sometimes dark coloured yarns are brittle and lacking in elasticity even when other colours in the same yarn knit easily. This is because of the amount of dye pigment which they have absorbed.

Buying yarns

Hand knitting yarns are mostly sold as 3 ply, 4 ply etc. to correspond with the requirements of knitting patterns. The number of plies does not necessarily indicate the weight and thickness of a yarn, as the individual strands may be thick or thin. For convenience, and so that knitting patterns may be written which are suitable for a wide range of standard sized yarns, the spinners of hand knitting yarns do use approximately the same thickness of singles yarn for doubling. Even so, manufacturers sometimes offer yarns which they state are equivalent to 4 ply, for example, but which are not actually made of four strands. This means that they are suitable to use with 4 ply patterns.

The range of hand knitting yarns available does not satisfy the needs of the machine knitter for several reasons. First of all, the tendency in hand knitting is towards thicker yarns because of the speed with which they are knitted. The finest yarn stocked by many wool shops is 4 ply, which is almost the thickest yarn which it is possible to knit in the normal way by machine. In machine knitting, which is so much faster than hand knitting, the time saved by using a thick yarn is insignificant.

The variety of fancy and textured yarns in hand knitting ranges is also limited, partly for the same reason: the need to standardise thicknesses. Also, the small balls in which hand knitting yarns are packed are unsuitable for machine knitting. They have to be rewound before knitting, and they are used up very quickly, which causes constant interruptions in order to make joins. Most important of all, yarns bought from retail shops are too expensive for the machine knitter, who uses them up so rapidly.

Most machine knitting patterns available are for 4 ply fingering, being the thinnest standardised yarn which is universally available. However there are not many machine knitting patterns available of any description, when compared to hand knitting patterns. This is partly because it is impossible to write a pattern which is suitable for all makes and models of machine. So to get the most from a knitting machine it is necessary to learn to work without a bought pattern, and this is not as difficult as it may seem, especially if a knit tracer is used. It is also much more rewarding to make something quite unique which you have designed yourself. Creating your own designs also overcomes the one drawback associated with buying wholesale yarns. That is that they are usually only available in minimum amounts of 1lb, which means that you often have to buy more than is needed for the job in hand. But if you are working out your own designs, there is no difficulty in incorporating left-over yarns in future work.

Yarns other than hand knitting yarns available to the machine knitter include yarns specially designed for the home machine knitter, industrial surplus knitting yarns, hand weaving yarns, industrial surplus weaving yarns, and such special items as ribbon, shirring elastic, and sewing and embroidery threads.

Yarn comes packed in various forms. It may be wound in hanks or skeins ready for dyeing, washing, or other finishing processes. If purchased in this form it must be wound into suitable balls, or onto cones, before knitting. Hand knitting yarns are packed in small balls. These too have to be rewound as they do not unwind freely enough for machine knitting.

Yarn intended specifically for machine knitting is supplied wound on cones from which the yarn will feed vertically with no drag. The smallest cones hold 6oz; the largest, for industrial use, hold 2lb. The labels inside cones of industrial yarn should be ignored as the cones are often re-used several times, and the label usually refers to the yarn that they had on them originally.

Weaving yarns come on straight tubes, or spools. It is possible to stand them on a board with a vertical peg to hold them upright and knit directly from them, but the yarn tends to drag and catch on the bottom of the spool. For textured or bulky yarn it is advisable to rewind before knitting.

There are many companies who specialise in supplying the home knitter by mail order with yarns on cones and in balls, and they frequently advertise in knitting magazines. There are also companies who supply yarns for hand weavers which are often of use to machine knitters. They advertise in weaving and craft magazines and are often listed in books on weaving. Industrial surplus yarns are available from mail order companies, from stalls in street markets, from knitting machine shops, and, if you are lucky enough to live near one, sometimes direct from a knitting factory or weaving mill. Mill shops, which sell small quantities of yarn not needed by the mill, are quite common in Scotland, and would be well worth a visit if you go there on holiday.

Some companies who are primarily suppliers to industry are willing to supply private purchasers with yarn if an order of a certain minimum value is received. For special effects, ribbon, shirring elastic, sewing and overlocking threads on cones are available from wholesale haberdashers. Some addresses in all these categories are listed at the back of the book.

Yarn sizes

The indication of the thickness or relative weight of yarns will seem very confusing at first. There are various systems by which it may be done.

The British system is in use in most English speaking countries, including the USA and Australia. There are usually two figures separated by an oblique stroke e.g. 2/6s (pronounced two sixes). The first figure tells how many ply the yarn is. The second figure indicates the weight of the singles yarn which has been plied. If there is one figure on its own e.g. 2s, it indicates a singles yarn of a certain weight. The second figure, which indicates the weight of the singles yarn, gives the number of hanks to the pound. The hanks are of a certain standard length, so the more hanks to the pound and the higher the number, the thinner the yarn will be. The standard length of hank varies from fibre to fibre. For cotton and silk it is 840 yards. For worsted it is 560 yards. For woollen yarn the length of the hank varies from region to region, but the most common length, originating in Yorkshire, is 256 yards. Yarns spun from staple man-made fibres use the hank length of the natural fibre they most resemble.

In Europe the same hank length of 1000 metres is used for all fibres. The count indicates the number of hanks in one kilogram. The ply number, in contrast to the British system, is written after the singles count e.g. 4/2 indicates a yarn of two ply made up of singles yarns which weigh 4000 metres to the kilogram.

For filament yarn a system is used which originated in the silk industry and was subsequently adopted for synthetic filament yarns. It is based on the unit of denier. The denier figure indicates the weight in grams of 9000 metres of yarn. The higher the number the thicker the yarn.

A standard international system of yarn measurement has been devised but has yet to be adopted widely by the textile industry. This system is called Tex. The Tex figure indicates the weight in grams of 1000 metres of yarn, e.g. 100 Tex means that 1000 metres weighs 100 gms. As in denier the higher the number the thicker the yarn.

The Basic Techniques

The most important rule to remember is – do not be in too much of a hurry. When you first start using your machine do everything slowly and carefully. There is no need to hurry. However slowly you work, it is still much faster than knitting by hand. If you try to knit too fast, the chances are that you will make a mistake, which will take much longer to put right than the whole operation would have taken if performed slowly. This is particularly important when casting on and knitting the first few rows. After that things will settle down and run smoothly without too much trouble.

Do not be discouraged if mistakes do occur. As you gain more experience, mistakes are less likely to happen, but they will still occur. However, you will learn to put them right quickly and with confidence.

Be patient in progressing from your first simple plain knitting to more adventurous stitches and patterns. Once the basic techniques of casting on, knitting plain, and casting off have been mastered, many interesting and attractive articles can be made. It is best to be content with the limitations imposed by a knowledge of the simplest techniques until you are quite confident and at ease with them, before attempting more difficult patterns.

The same approach should be applied to the shapes of articles to be knitted. There are lots of interesting things to be made from simple squares and rectangles while you are still getting to know the machine. Complicated shaping and patterning can be left until a later date when you are quite confident of the basic techniques. The techniques and methods described in this chapter are the same for all machines, from the simplest to the most complex.

Preparing yarn

It is absolutely essential that yarn fed to the tensioner is free running with no sudden snagging or dragging. Unevenness in the flow of yarn to the carriage accounts for most of the jamming, dropped stitches, and other mishaps. There are two ways for yarn to be wound so that it will unwind freely: on cones, or in special machine knitting balls. All yarn which is not purchased on cones should be rewound into balls on one of the ball winders available from machine manufacturers.

Skeins and hanks are most easily wound into balls if they are first placed on a skein holder which will allow the yarn to unwind freely. Metal skein holders are available from knitting machine suppliers and wooden ones from hand weaving suppliers. The skein should be placed on the holder which is then adjusted to hold the skein taut before any of the ties on the skein are undone. If the skein is untied first there is a danger that it will not unwind freely.

Alternatively the skein may be stretched across the hands of a helper. If no helper is available, it is possible to wind a skein which has been stretched over the back of a chair, or for larger skeins, round the legs of an upturned chair. The yarn must be unwound a turn at a time by hand before winding on. It will not work pulling the skein round and round the legs.

It is important, if one of these stop gap methods is used, to have the skein fairly taut, otherwise it will become tangled on itself and be very difficult to unwind. For regular use of skeined yarn, a skein holder is essential. The alternative methods are not only very slow but result in unevenly wound balls, which in turn will result in uneven knitting. If balls are particularly uneven, that is, tighter in some parts than others, it may be necessary to rewind them a second time before knitting.

It is possible to knit straight from tubes if a stand which will hold them vertical is made. The stand consists of a flat wooden base with a vertical post of dowel, or even a large nail, over which the tube fits. The yarn will then feed vertically. There is a danger of the yarn catching on the underside of the tube, so

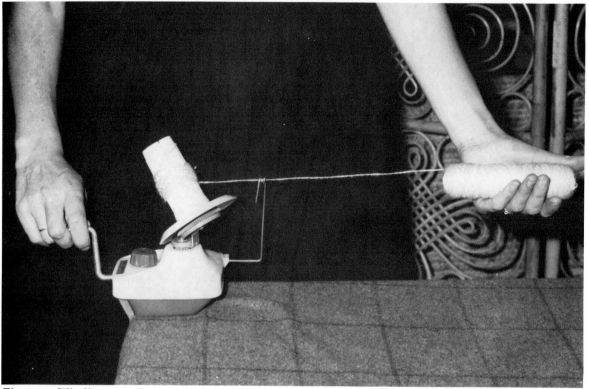

Figure 24 Winding yarn from a spool

special care must be taken when using this method. Also, the nearer the centre, the less easily the yarn will unwind, and it may be necessary to rewind the centre section into a ball before knitting. Spool racks are supplied by weaving suppliers to hold spools while they are being rewound. An alternative method is to hold the spool in the palm of the hand, level with and pointing towards the eye of the ball winder. The yarn will then pull off the end of the spool quite freely, without the spool jumping or rolling around (fig. 24).

When rewinding hand knitting balls it is a good idea to put them in a container first to prevent them running round the floor and tangling on furniture legs. The container might be a cardboard box with a hole in the lid for the yarn to pull through, a paper bag with the top screwed up to allow the yarn end but not the whole ball through, or even a large jar.

All yarns will knit more evenly and smoothly and require less physical effort to move the carriage if they are waxed. For many yarns it is essential to wax before knitting. Paraffin wax is used, which is available in small blocks from machine suppliers, or pieces of ordinary candle may be used. The method is simple. Hold the wax in the palm of your free hand whilst winding, and allow the yarn to pass

lightly over it before reaching the eye of the winder. Do not press the yarn against the wax. Only a very light waxing is necessary, and by pressing on the yarn you will make the ball wind too tightly. By the time the yarn is knitted there will be no trace of wax left. The wax will have rubbed off and helped to lubricate the feeder eyes and the needles.

Yarns which persistently snag or break will benefit from being rewound and waxed several times before knitting. This may seem very time consuming but in the long run will save time, as it prevents constant hold ups and mistakes in the knitting.

Another way of dealing with very difficult yarns is to oil them with a light machine oil spray before knitting. The oil must be washed out after knitting and before blocking. Synthetic yarns on cones usually knit quite smoothly without waxing. Some coned yarns, particularly wool, will require waxing. This can be done without rewinding by occasionally rubbing the wax down the outside layer of yarn on the cone. If too much pressure is applied when this is done, the lay of the yarn will be disturbed, and the yarn will not feed quite smoothly for several rows. With yarns prone to snagging or breaking it will be worthwhile rewinding the whole cone into balls to be sure of waxing the yarn thoroughly.

If large cones are used the machine must be set up on a narrow knitting table so that the cone can be placed on the floor for the yarn to run freely (fig. 25). If large cones are placed at table level the yarn is fed into the first feeder eye at too acute an angle and will snag on the top edge of the cone (fig. 26). If a narrow table is not available, large cones must be rewound.

A first exercise

This is a good way of becoming familiar with the machine and its workings before starting machine knitting proper. Set the main part of the machine, that is, the needle bed, on the table. Most machines clamp to the edge of the table, angled slightly upwards. This is to help prevent dropped stitches. The machine will be packed with the carriage on the needle bed; it will be held fast by a locking plate. Remove this according to the instructions in the machine's manual. Now slide the carriage off one end of the needle bed, and place it on one side. Do not yet unpack or set up the yarn tensioning unit.

Make sure the machine is in a good light. The best position is at right angles to a window or other source of light so that the light is coming from one side. If the light source is behind or above, you will block your own light. If it is in front, then the machine will block the light. Choose a light-coloured yarn so that you can easily see the stitches as they form; 3 or 4 ply pure wool is easy to knit. Place the ball of yarn on the floor in front of the machine.

Push all the needle butts back to position 'A' on the needle bed. Now bring 10 needles in the centre of the bed towards you as far as they will go. The needle butts will now be at position 'D' or 'E' depending on the model of machine. Take the end of yarn from the centre of the ball and make a slip knot in it (fig. 27). Place the loop over the first forward needle on the left. Push the loop as close to the needle bed as possible, that is, against the sinker gate. Pull the loop smaller but not tight on the needle. Now wind the yarn round each needle from left to right passing the yarn under each needle first, that is, anti-clockwise (fig. 28).

Make the loops loose enough to pass over the closed latch hook easily. Make sure that all the latches on the working needles are open. Pass the yarn back across the first right-hand needle inside its hook. With your other hand pull the butt of this needle back until the casting-on loop has dropped off and a new stitch has been formed as in figure 4.

Continue making new stitches and dropping the casting-on loops across all 10 needles. You have now

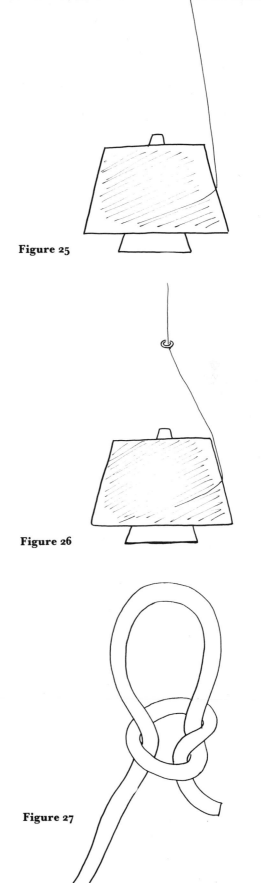

Figure 25

Figure 26

Figure 27

33

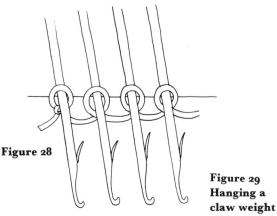

Figure 28

**Figure 29
Hanging a
claw weight**

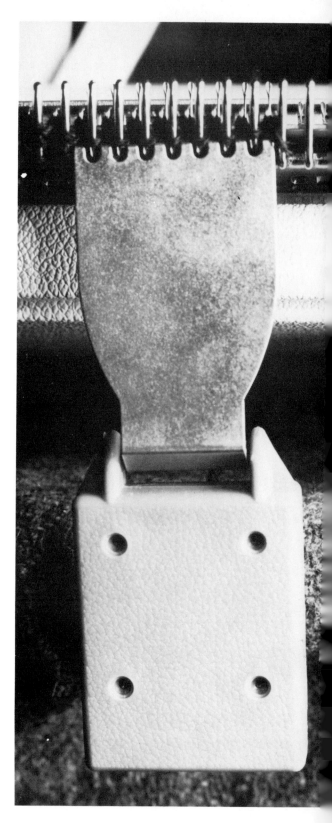

imitated the action of the machine in knitting one row. One hand has acted as the yarn tensioner and feeder. The other hand has controlled the movement of the needles in place of the cam box, which is the working part of the carriage. Hang a claw weight in the first row of knitting to help the old stitches to drop down (fig. 29).

Knit another row or two in the same way until you are quite familiar with the process. The size of stitch is determined by how far back the needle is pulled. Figure 30 shows a row of tight stitches and the first stitch of a loose row. The further back the needle is pulled, the bigger the stitch.

Using this method it is possible to imitate all the variations of stitch possible in machine knitting. The simplest variation is to knit only alternate stitches, thus forming floats in place of the missed stitches. This is slip stitch, which is shown in figure 13. See if you can imitate the other stitch variations illustrated in the first chapter, or even think up some variations of your own. To remove the knitting from the machine, bring all the needles right forward, pull down on the knitting, and pull the needles sharply back.

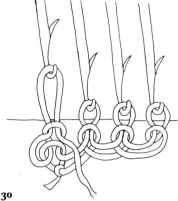

Figure 30

Threading

The basic layout of the yarn tensioner (fig. 31) is common to all machines. It is set on a stainless steel rod fixed almost vertically at the back of the needle bed. There are four points through which the yarn must be threaded, and on some machines five points, before the yarn is finally led to the carriage. The ball of yarn is placed on the table behind the machine.

The first eye (1) through which it must be threaded is about halfway up the steel rod on an arm which extends backwards so that the yarn may be led exactly vertically to it. It is important to place the ball immediately below this first eye, otherwise the tension on the yarn will vary and may cause irregularities in the knitting.

The yarn is then led to the top of the rod and through a tensioning disk (2) similar to a sewing machine tensioner. Be sure to pass the yarn inside the peg at the back of the disk to prevent it from jumping out of the spring while knitting is in progress.

The next eye (3) is at the forward end of the cross piece, which is at the top of the vertical rod. Then the yarn is led to an eye at the end of the antenna spring (4) which is bent forward from the top of the rod. On some machines the yarn is led from this fourth eye to the carriage. On others there is a fifth eye (5), forward of eye 3, from which the yarn is led to the carriage.

The tension disk at 2 can be adjusted according to the thickness of the yarn. It is possible to thread two separate yarns at the same time, one at either side of the tensioner, for knitting fairisle or two coloured stripes. On some machines it is possible to set up a second rod and so have four yarns threaded up ready for use at one time.

Casting on

There are four ways to cast on: closed cast on by hand, open cast on, and two ways of making mechanical closed cast ons. A closed cast on is one that will not unravel. A closed cast on by hand gives a firm solid edge. A closed cast on done mechanically gives a loose but secure edge.

Whenever it is necessary to move the needles backwards and forwards it is done by pushing the needle butts. To begin with it is easiest to do it with your finger. To move several needles at once, the side of the hand or finger may be used. With practice, it is quicker to use the needle pushers supplied with the machine.

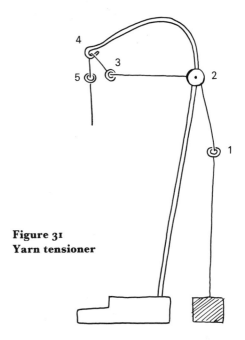

Figure 31
Yarn tensioner

Closed cast on by hand

This is the method already described on page 33. However this time the yarn tensioner must first be set up and the carriage replaced on the needle bed, with the sinker plate attached to it. Rest the carriage on the right-hand side of the needle bed. The number of needles required to knit should be brought forward in the centre of the needle bed. Make sure that all the remaining needles are right back in the non-knitting position.

Thread the yarn on the tensioner as already described. Bring the yarn down into the yarn feed in the centre of the sinker plate. On machines with two feeder positions, use the number one feeder nearest the needle bed. There will be either a spring or a gate behind which the yarn must pass. If the yarn is not behind it, stitches will not form. Tie a slip knot in the end of the yarn and place the loop on the left-hand forward needle. Pull plenty of slack yarn down through the yarn feed and then wrap loosely round each of the forward needles (fig. 28).

It is important to have the yarn slack, not pulled taut by the tensioner, when casting on. If it is not, the casting on will be too tight, and the carriage will jam on the first row. When the casting on is completed, take up the slack by pulling down on the yarn just below the number one feeder.

Set all the controls on the machine at neutral or as for plain knitting. Set the stitch size dial in the centre of the carriage at one number looser than normal for the thickness of yarn. For 4 ply hand knitting yarn the normal tension would be 8 or 9. For fine yarns that require a very low stitch size, select several numbers higher for the casting on. Slide the carriage until it is almost in contact with the first needle in the knitting position, and at the same time take up any remaining slack by pulling the yarn upwards just above the sinker plate.

Pass the carriage from right to left across the knitting needles. Move the carriage slowly and easily and stop as soon as the carriage has cleared the last needle. Just at the point when you should stop the carriage there is a temptation to speed up, as the carriage feels lighter once the needles have been cleared. If you do finish the row with a burst of speed it will pull the last few stitches tighter than they should be, and they are then likely to jam on the next row. Also the yarn in the feeder will be too loose at the beginning of the next row resulting in loops at the edge and perhaps dropped stitches.

If the carriage jams on the first row, the casting on loops were too tight. If stitches are dropped or do not form properly, the casting on loops were too loose. Now set the stitch size dial to the normal number for the thickness of yarn and continue knitting slowly and at a regular speed. It is important to keep an eye not only on the needles, to make sure that there are no snags or problems, but also on the yarn tensioner, to make sure there are no knots or breakages higher up.

If the carriage jams or feels stiff or anything else seems wrong, stop immediately. Never reverse the direction of the carriage in the middle of a row or damage to the machine will result. Undo the thumb screws which hold the sinker plate to the carriage and slide the sinker plate off. Lift the carriage up from the needle bed slightly at the front and slide it back to the beginning of the row. On some machines this is not possible, in which case there will be a release lever which makes it possible to lift the carriage completely clear of the needle bed.

Unpick the stitches back to the beginning of the row. Check for knots or overtight stitches on the previous row. If everything seems normal take up the slack through the tensioner and replace the sinker plate on the carriage. Continue knitting. If the carriage jams on the first row after casting on, then the casting-on loops were too tight. Remove the loops from the needles and cast on a second time, more loosely, before continuing knitting.

If, when the carriage is passed across the needles on the first row after casting on, the needles do not move at all, slide the carriage back to the right-hand side. Check the hold position levers or switch. Whether there are one or two and their exact

position on the carriage will depend on the model of machine. Make sure they are set to the knit in position. This is the normal knitting position. Continue knitting.

If the casting on row falls off when the first row is knitted then the yarn was not threaded correctly in the sinker plate feeder. Re-thread and start again.

Open cast on

This is also best done with the stitch size dial set to a slightly higher number than normal for the type of yarn. Bring the number of needles required to the forward position. Thread the yarn in the sinker plate feeder, and tie the end to the table leg or machine clamp. When you are a little more experienced you will be able to dispense with tying the end of the yarn. It may be held below the machine with your free hand.

Knit one row. This first row of open loops must be held down on the needles while the next few rows are knitted. This can be done in one of two ways. Brother machines are supplied with a casting on comb, which is a row of hooks attached to a weighted bar. A hook is attached to the yarn between each needle, and the weight of the bar prevents the loops jumping off the needles while the first row is knitted.

Other machines are supplied with a strong nylon cord. After the first row is knitted this is placed across the loops between the needles and the sinker gate. The sinker gate is the row of pegs along the front of the needle bed. The two ends of the cord are held together and pulled down with the free hand while the next two or three rows are knitted. Then the cord is pulled out and knitting is continued.

It is difficult to pull the cord down hard enough if thick yarn is being used or if the casting on is over a large number of needles. It is easier to do if the two ends of the cord are crossed and pulled tightly together, and then gripped tightly with the thumb on the cross to prevent the cord slipping (fig. 32).

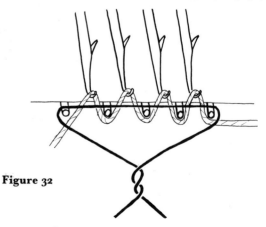

Figure 32

Even so, when the second row has been knitted, there may be some stitches which have not knitted over the top of the cord. If there are not too many of them and you continue to pull hard on the cord they will probably knit over the cord on the third row. If there are too many stitches which have not knitted over the cord, the carriage will jam on the third row. In this case it is necessary to remove the yarn from the needles and start from the beginning again.

If the special cord is not available, any reasonably strong smooth yarn may be used in its place. If the cord is not pulled out soon enough after casting on has been completed, the first row will remain caught up on the sinker pegs. This will not prevent you from continuing knitting. The fabric will hang down in a fold from the machine. When the knitting has been completed and removed from the needles, the bottom edge may be lifted off the pegs and the knitting will be unharmed.

Mechanical closed cast on

The first method is the simplest. Bring alternate needles to the forward position. Keep the remaining needles in the non-knitting position. Thread and secure the end of the yarn. Knit one row. Bring the empty needles up to the 'B' position in line with those already knitting. Continue knitting. Some difficult yarns may snarl up on the second row. If so, proceed as follows. Knit one row on alternate needles. Lay the cord across as in open cast on. Bring the empty needles to the knitting position. Pull down the ends of the cord with your free hand. Knit several rows. Pull the cord out, and continue knitting.

The second method is carried out as follows. Bring all the needles required to the knitting position, i.e. 'B' position. Do not bring them all the way forward for this method. If you have a punch card machine, place card number 1 with the 1 × 1 bird's eye pattern in the machine. Before threading the yarn, pass the carriage across the needles twice to line them up and to feed in the pattern. Thread the yarn and secure it below the knitting table.

Set the carriage to knit slip stitch. On manual or button selection machines, select odd needles to knit. Knit one row. Then select even needles to knit. Knit one row. Repeat this sequence one more time. Change the settings to plain knitting. Continue knitting. Note that on some machines slip stitch buttons are marked 'part' or 'empty'.

Uses for various cast ons

Most machine knitted fabrics are naturally curly.

However carefully they are steamed flat, the edge will gradually curl up again, and so in practice edges which are not seamed are turned or hemmed, so that a cast on edge very rarely shows in a finished piece of work. The exception is the ribbed edge which is naturally firm and flat and does not require turning. The open cast on is quick to do, and is suitable for sample swatches and design ideas. If you want to keep the swatch, steaming will minimise the tendency to unravel, and a strip of adhesive tape or a dab of glue along the edge will make it quite secure.

Open edges are desirable where knitting is started with waste yarn which must be unravelled at a later stage. Mechanical closed cast on edges are best when casting on a wide piece of knitting, as both the open and hand cast on are difficult to do over a large number of needles. The mechanical cast ons are more elastic than a hand cast on, and so are more suitable for use in seams where it is desirable to have as much elasticity in the seam as in the body of the knitting.

Where a hem has to be stitched after the knitting has been removed from the machine (as when the technical reverse side of the fabric is used) mechanical cast ons are quicker to pick up than an open edge, but do not make as much of a bump as hand cast on edges, which may show through to the right side. It is best to practise casting on by hand first, and when you are quite confident about it, go on to practise the other methods.

Casting (binding) off

The simplest way to remove knitting from the machine is to remove the yarn from the sinker plate feeder, and knit one row with the feeder empty. The knitting will fall off. This will give an edge which will unravel if pulled, but it is fast to do, and may be used for the same purposes and in the same way as already described for the open cast on.

Knitted cast off

This method of casting off involves the use of the transfer tool which is explained on page 42. Before trying this method of casting off, it is best to practise the simple use of the transfer tool as described there. If you are right-handed, you will find it easiest if you stop knitting with the carriage on the left-hand side. Transfer the first stitch on the left to the second needle. There are now two stitches on the second needle. Holding the knitting close to the needle bed with the left hand, bring the second needle to the forward position by pushing its butt with the right hand. Pull enough yarn down through the feeder so that the spring is no longer holding it under tension.

Now bring the yarn across into the hook of the needle and pull the needle back to knit a new stitch. This is the same action already described on page 33. The only difference is that in this case two stitches are being knitted into one. One stitch has been cast off.

Repeat this process of transferring a stitch and then knitting two into one across the whole width of the knitting until there is only one stitch left. Knit this stitch into itself once, break the yarn off, and pull the knitting down sharply so that the end of the yarn is pulled up through the loop of the stitch. The casting off is now secured and will not unravel.

It is easy to cast off too tightly so that the knitting is gathered at the top. To avoid this, ensure the yarn has been pulled down sufficiently and is not still under tension from the spring, and make large stitches when casting off by pulling the needle well back. It also helps to change to a looser tension on the last row before casting off. Another way of making sure that the cast off edge is not pulling in is to transfer either the first stitch or all the stitches behind the sinker peg instead of in front of it (fig. 33).

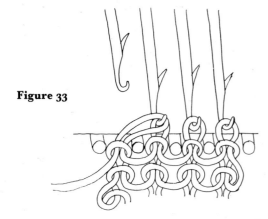

Figure 33

Crocheted cast off
This method is a little trickier to do at first, but is very quick once it has been mastered. It is not suitable for thicker yarns with which it will cast off too tightly. Before knitting the last row change to a stitch size several numbers higher. The latch tool is required for this job. It is a tool with a latch hook identical to those on the knitting needles on the machine, but with a plastic handle and no butt. If one is not available, a spare knitting needle will do just as well, although it is not as comfortable to hold.

Start from the opposite side from the carriage.

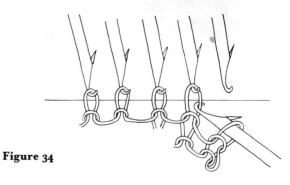

Figure 34

Pull the knitting downwards with the left hand and insert the tool into the stitch on the first needle and hook it onto this stitch. Still holding down the knitting, keep the tool in place with the left hand. With the right hand, push the needle forward, and then back, so dropping the stitch from the needle and leaving it on the latch hook. Push the tool so that the stitch slips behind the latch. Transfer the next stitch to the hook of the tool in the same way (fig. 34).

Pull the tool towards you so the first stitch is dropped and the second stitch remains in the hook. Repeat this process until the last stitch is on the latch tool. Insert the yarn into the hook and drop the stitch. Break the yarn and pull the end through the last stitch to secure the casting off.

Straight thread cast off
This method does not give a very neat edge but has the advantages that it is quick to do, and it gives an edge which has as much elasticity as the body of the knitting. Finish with the carriage on the right. Break the yarn off allowing about 5 centimetres (2 inches) more than the width of the knitting. Thread the end of the yarn into a blunt knitwear sewing needle. Insert the needle into the first four or five stitches underneath the needles (fig. 35).

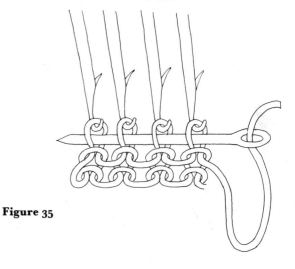

Figure 35

Bring these needles forward and then back to drop the stitches. Repeat on the next group of needles and continue until all the stitches are gathered on the straight yarn. Secure the end. A neater edge is achieved by knitting the last row at a relatively tight tension, although it will not be so elastic.

Trouble-free knitting

Most things that go wrong are caused by the tensioner not working properly. The carriage itself rarely gives trouble. So it is important to keep an eye on the tensioner to see that the yarn is going through properly. The most important way of ensuring that the tensioner feeds the yarn at a constant tension is to avoid jogging or any other erratic movement of the carriage. Move the carriage at a constant speed, and only far enough at the end of the row to just clear the needles.

The antenna spring should be pulled about half-way down by the yarn when knitting. If it is too high it means the yarn is being fed to the needles too loosely. If it is too low the yarn is being fed too tightly. Adjustment to the disk tensioner will usually remedy the problem.

Very thin or slippery yarn should be wound round the disk tensioner twice to increase tension. Thick or textured yarn may have to be pulled down through the antenna spring by hand at the end of each row to prevent it from becoming too tight. Other bulky yarns will knit too loosely at the beginning of a row because the spring is not strong enough to take up the slack yarn from underneath the carriage as it is brought into contact with the first needle of the row. This results in dropped stitches, loops at the edge of the fabric, or slack yarn becoming entangled in the sinker plate brushes and jamming the carriage.

All these may be avoided by holding the yarn just above the sinker plate with your free hand, and as the carriage is brought towards the knitting, pulling the slack yarn up through the feeder. Let go as soon as the yarn comes into contact with the first needle. The yarn will become taut again at this point. By keeping an eye on the yarn as it runs through the tensioner you will also notice knots, snags, break-ages or the end of the yarn before any damage is done.

Snags and knots may catch at any point passing through the tensioner, causing the yarn to knit too tightly and eventually to break. If they pass through as far as the needles they may jam the carriage, cause broken yarn and dropped stitches. If the knot or tangle cannot be undone it should be cut off and the new end joined as described on page 40. If the end of the yarn is reached without it being noticed, the knitting will drop completely off the needles.

The use of claw weights is not always necessary. When they are used they are hooked into the knitting at the edges. They help to prevent edge stitches dropping off, which is sometimes a problem. It is advisable to use them when knitting thick yarns, as the stitches do not drop down as easily, causing accidental tuck stitches. When this is a particular problem it may be necessary to pull the fabric down by hand at the end of each row.

If work is to be left half finished on the machine, the weights should be removed and the weight of the knitting taken off the needle by placing it on a chair under the needle bed. If this is not done, a permanent mark may result from the row of stitches on the needles being overstretched. Use of weights is advisable when casting off or transferring stitches and for tuck and slip patterns.

The importance of placing the machine in a good light has already been stressed. The importance of approaching the machine in a good mood must also be emphasised. Successful machine knitting requires alertness and attention to detail. It is impossible to do when you are tired or distraught. This is particularly the case when problems arise. If, after one or two attempts, the problem cannot be overcome, it is best to leave the machine altogether for a while and to come back to it later when refreshed. Knitting machines seem to respond to sympathy, and to baulk at bad-tempered handling. The idea of machines being responsive to the way they are handled is borne out by the fact that machines which are always used by the same person seem to go on forever without requiring attention, whereas those used by many different people, as in colleges for example, are constantly breaking down.

It is a good idea, if the machine is to be left clamped on its table, to make a loose fabric dust cover to put over it when not in use. After each session, brush out all the dust and fluff from the needle bed, particularly from between the needles. Slide the carriage off the needle bed and brush the underneath thoroughly. Any yarn wound round the brushes or wheels must be removed. There is a brush for this purpose in most machine tool kits. Manufacturers' manuals recommend oiling after every use, but it is easy to over-oil, causing clogging and soiling of knitting. Occasional oiling is sufficient. Light machine oil may be used. Brother supplies a lubricating cream which will not stain work.

Needle beds on all machines have two sets of markings. Starting at o in the centre of the bed they are numbered in groups of ten to right and left, with intermediate marks for every fifth needle. The second set of marks shows where the centre and the edge of each pattern repeat is. How far apart these are spaced depends on the number of stitches in each pattern repeat for the particular machine.

Symmetrical shapes, e.g. the back of a cardigan, are knitted at the centre of the needle bed, bringing out exactly half of the total needles required on either side of the o in the centre. Asymmetrical shapes, e.g. the front of a cardigan, are knitted to the right or the left of centre line, starting with needle 1 on the appropriate side. If this procedure is always followed, the numbers marked on the bed will always correspond to the number of stitches required. This will avoid a lot of unnecessary counting, and will make it very simple to match patterns and stripes across seams etc.

Design in plain knitting

This heading may seem a contradiction in terms, but there certainly are many design decisions to be made, even in plain knitting. The first and most important is the choice of yarn or yarns, which has been discussed in detail in an earlier chapter.

Stitch size
The next decision is the choice of stitch size in relation to the particular yarn. There are no hard and fast rules about this. It is a matter of trying different stitch sizes until the required effect is achieved. A common mistake is to choose a stitch size which produces a fabric which is too heavy or inflexible. The small sample swatch always seems lighter and more open than knitting at the same stitch size over larger areas. This is because it is easier to stretch the small swatch when handling it, and because light shows through, making it seem more open.

A better guide than what the swatch looks like is what it feels like, whether it will drape or gather as required, and whether it will be comfortable to wear. You must finish the swatch in the same way that the finished work is to be finished before a decision can be made. For most yarns this means steaming, which will have the effect of flattening the fabric, making it more opaque. Washing may add bulk. If yarns of different types of fibre are used together it is wise to wash the swatch to see that they react in a compatible way.

If several stitch sizes are tried out in one continuous length of knitting, the sections should be separated by a single row of extra loose or extra

tight knitting. Interesting effects are possible by knitting different tensions in the same fabric. This will of course result in stripes of tight and loose knitting, but may also cause an undulating surface effect too. Either keep a note book by the machine and record the stitch sizes of samples, or label them as you go along. It is impossible to remember the exact stitch sizes of particular swatches after having tried out several.

Knitting on selected needles only will result in ladder or rib effects, or looser knitting, depending on the type of yarn used. It is simply done. Bring the needles out to the knitting position for the width required. Then push back every third, fourth, or any other sequence of needles, to the non-knitting position before casting on. It will be necessary to knit on selected needles only, if yarn thicker than 4 ply is used, as otherwise it will produce an extremely stiff fabric and be very hard to knit. If a rib effect is not wanted, select every alternate needle.

Striping
Striping may be used with plain or any of the pattern stitches. It may be used to produce a contrast of colour, yarn texture, thickness, or a combination of all three. Different thickness of yarns will produce a ripple effect, but this may be lost in finishing. Most machines have provision for carrying only two yarns at a time through the tensioner, so we will deal with two colour striping first.

The two yarns are threaded one on either side of the tensioner. One yarn is secured at the clip at the front of the main rod of the tensioner. If there is no clip, tie a loose slip knot at the last eye of the tensioner. The other yarn is used to cast on and commence knitting. When the second yarn is to be introduced, the first yarn is slipped out of the yarn feed and hooked over the end of the needle bed.

Move the carriage slightly as the yarn is removed from the feeder to make sure that it has completely cleared the sinker plate wheels and brushes. The second yarn is threaded in the yarn feed, the end is secured below the machine, and knitting is continued. It is only practical to knit even numbers of rows in each yarn. If one row of each yarn were knitted, for example, the yarn would have to be broken at the end of each row and taken across to the opposite side of the machine.

There are two ways of knitting stripes of three or more yarns. If large block stripes are knitted, it is easiest to break off one of the yarns already threaded and replace it with the next yarn required. If small stripes of several yarns are required this procedure would become tedious. In this case, the balls of extra

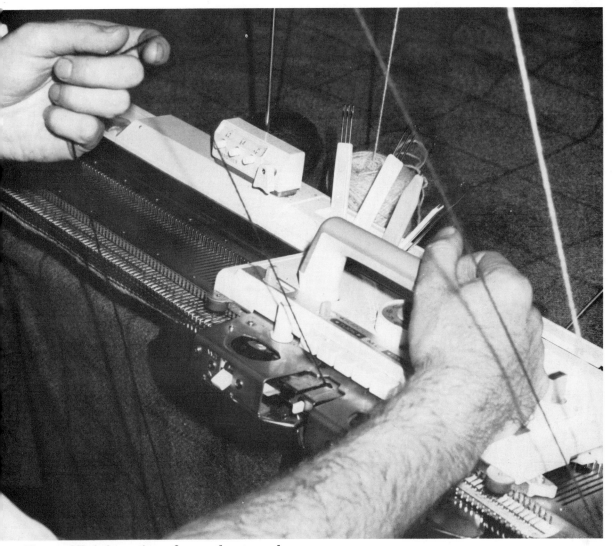

Figure 36 Knitting stripes of more than two colours

yarn are placed on the floor in front of the machine. When it is time to knit with one of the yarns on the floor, both the threaded up yarns are hooked round the end of the machine. The end of the new yarn is tied to the table leg or machine clamp, and then threaded into the yarn feed on the sinker plate. It is then held lightly above the carriage with your free hand (fig. 36).

Continue knitting, allowing the yarn to slip freely over the left hand. If the yarn is held too tightly you will feel a tug, and you must let out more yarn before finishing the row. At the beginning of each row the slack must be taken up as the carriage is brought towards the first needle, to avoid loops and tangling. As soon as you feel the first needle pulling at the yarn, let it run freely again.

When you have finished knitting the stripe, unclip the yarn from the feeder and let it drop down. Then thread either one of the yarns in the tensioner or another yarn from the floor. On punch card machines, striping is slower to do than any pattern fabric because of all the yarn changing.

Colour changer attachments, which are available for some models, speed up the process considerably. They hold up to four yarns ready threaded, and any one of the four may be selected to knit at the press of a button. They may be used in pattern as well as plain knitting, so speeding up the production of multi-coloured fairisle, tuck, and slip patterns.

On machines with a plating feeder, if a thick yarn is threaded in one feeder, and a thin yarn in the other, single stripes will result automatically.

The transfer tool

The transfer tool, as its name suggests, is designed to pick up stitches from one needle and transfer them to another. It is used in casting off, increasing and decreasing, and for decorative effects such as lace stitches and pick up tuck. It is important when using the transfer tool to hold it properly. It must be horizontal and at right angles to the needle bed, i.e. in line with the needle. This is easier to do if it is held underhand like a frying pan, not overhand like a pen. Hook the eye of the tool onto the hook of the needle. If the needle latch is closed, push the eye of the tool onto the top of the needle keeping it horizontal, and the latch will be pushed open (fig. 37).

With your free hand hold the knitting down and against the machine (fig. 38). Pull the transfer tool sharply towards you, bringing the needle with it, and leaving the stitch behind the latch. Push the tool away from you with the needle still attached. The latch will close and the stitch will slip onto the transfer tool. Hook the transfer tool onto the next needle and tip it upwards until the stitch slips onto the new needle (fig. 39).

If you continue knitting with the empty needle back in its normal knitting position, a hole will be left in the fabric. This is the basis of lace patterns. If the empty needle is returned to the non-knitting position a ladder effect is created. The empty needle may be brought into the knitting position at any time to close the ladder and resume solid knitting. This technique may be used in designs on its own, combined with normal lace stitch, or with tuck stitch to make another type of lace effect.

To make a long tuck stitch with the transfer tool, insert the tool into a stitch several rows down. Transfer the stitch from the tool to the needle above. Continue knitting. If stitches are picked up across the whole width of the knitting, a ripple or fold will result.

Figure 37

Figure 38

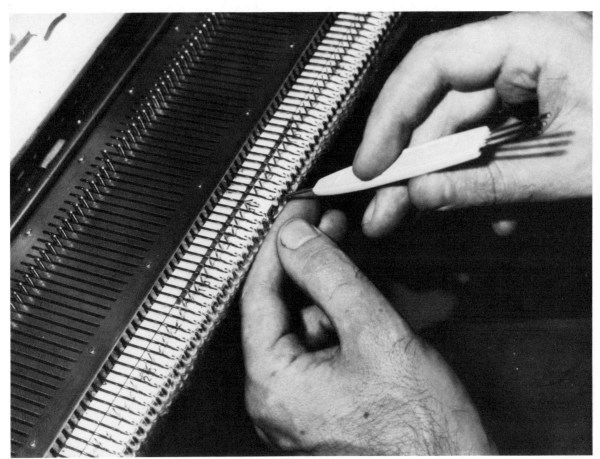

Figure 39

Creating Fabrics

Fabric quality

The importance of the selection and combination of yarns, and of stitch size to design and fabric quality has already been mentioned. Basic stitch variations have been shown in the first chapter. They are normally thought of as being ways of adding a decorative element to the knitting, but they also contribute to the physical quality, and therefore to the suitability of the fabric for particular purposes. An example already mentioned is the use of fancy stitches to bulk up a fabric made of a particularly thin yarn.

All-over tuck stitch produces a bulky, non-curling fabric with fewer stitches than normal. The bulk makes it a warm fabric. The lack of curl makes it easy to make up and means that edges do not necessarily have to be turned or finished in any way. Because tuck stitches spread widthways, particularly wide panels may be knitted.

Slip stitch makes an opaque fabric with little stretch. Fairisle is softer than plain knitting. Woven or inlay fabrics have little lateral stretch and may be cut with little danger of unravelling. These are just some of the variations possible using plain yarns and simple stitches. By exploiting a selection of yarns and stitches in this way, anything from a slinky evening dress to a thick fireside rug may be made.

Stitch pattern controls

Although the layout may vary, all punch card machines have the same simple set of controls, which are as follows.

Pattern card controls

Next to the slot for the pattern card is a knob for rolling the card round manually, and a switch to set the card to roll automatically as knitting progresses or to hold the card still so that the same pattern row is knitted over and over. Most machines have a third position for this switch which makes the card roll down only every other row, so knitting each pattern row twice. There is a control which engages and disengages the needles from the pattern card. This is usually a knob on top of the carriage, but on the Knitmaster and Studio it consists of a lever on either side of the carriage.

Stitch selection

The control for selecting which type of fancy stitch is to be knitted is placed centrally on the carriage, with positions for plain, tuck, slip, and fairisle. Slip stitch may alternatively be labelled 'part' or 'empty'. Fairisle may be labelled 'two colour', or 'multi-colour (MC)'. There are sometimes duplicate controls. One selects the stitch when knitting from left to right and the other selects the stitch when knitting from right to left.

If a row or two of plain knitting is required in the middle of pattern knitting, the stitch selector may simply be changed to plain. If a large area of plain knitting is to be done, the needles should be disengaged from the pattern card as well, to avoid unnecessary mechanical movement which makes the carriage heavier to operate. When changing back to pattern knitting the needles should be engaged with the pattern card and one row knitted with the stitch selector still on plain, before changing over to pattern knitting. This is necessary because the pattern needles are pre-selected. This row selects the needles for the first row of the pattern.

Other controls and attachments

There will be a second feeder position in front of the main one for the second yarn needed to knit fairisle. As mentioned in the previous chapter there is a centrally situated control marked from 1 to 10 to select stitch size. Number 1 is the tightest stitch and 10 is the loosest.

For weaving, the stitch selector is set to plain, but the pattern card is engaged. The weaving yarn is controlled by a pair of brushes set in the top of the sinker plate. They must be in the lowered position to come in contact with the needles, when in use. When not in use they are removed from the carriage or hinged up out of contact with the needles, depending on the machine. The knitting yarn is threaded on one side of the tensioner and into the yarn feed on the sinker plate. The laying in yarn is threaded on the other side of the tensioner, taken in front of the carriage, i.e. on the side nearest the knitting, and the end tied off below the machine.

Knitmaster and Studio have a hook with a red knob on either side of the sinker plate inside which the yarn must pass. As the row is knitted the laying in yarn is pushed in front of the carriage by a 'V' shaped groove in the sinker plate. At the end of each row the laying-in yarn is brought round to the opposite side of the carriage, so that it is again between the sinker plate and the knitting. Slide the carriage at the same time as transferring the laying in yarn from one side to the other, moving it slowly away from the knitting. This prevents the yarn tangling on the wheels and brushes of the sinker plate.

Lace knitting is carried out in the same way on all models except Knitmaster and Studio. As with weaving, the pattern card is engaged but the stitch selector is set to plain. Before each row is knitted the lace carriage, which carries out the transfer of stitches from selected needles, is passed across the needle bed.

The remaining control, which consists either of a pair of levers marked with roman numerals and set one on either side of the carriage, or a single control on the top of the carriage, has already been mentioned in describing methods of casting on. This control is variously labelled 'holding cam', 'returning', or 'partial knitting'. Their normal position is at knit in. Then, if needles are brought forward of the normal knitting position, e.g. in casting on by hand, they will automatically knit back to the knitting position when a row is knitted. If they are set to hold, needles in the forward position will not knit when the carriage is passed across them, making is possible to knit one section of stitches while at the same time holding another section. This facility has many applications.

Non punch card models

The various ways of selecting pattern stitches have already been described. All machines however, have similar controls for selecting which type of stitch is to be knitted. Some will not have weaving brushes. None will have a second feeder for the extra yarn in fairisle. The second yarn will have to be either laid across the needles by hand at the beginning of each row, or fed in front of the sinker plate as in weaving; alternatively fairisle effects may be achieved by knitting slip stitch patterns combined with striping.

Needle selection

As already mentioned, patterns on punch card machines are pre-selected. On all but Knitmaster and Studio models, this means that the selected needles are automatically brought to a forward position before a row is knitted. Selected needles correspond to positions on the pattern card where a hole has been punched.

If a pattern stitch is selected but the card is disengaged, the needles will act as if all positions on the pattern card are blanks. For example, on slip stitch it is possible to pass the carriage across with no movement of the needles. If a pattern stitch is selected, and the pattern card is engaged, but there is no card in the slot, all needles will act as if all positions on the card are holes. How holes and blank spaces relate to particular stitches is shown below.

STITCH	HOLES IN PATTERN CARD	BLANK SPACE ON PATTERN CARD
tuck	plain	tuck
slip	plain	slip
fairisle	second colour	main colour
lace	lace	plain
weave	float	weave in

On non punch card machines, selected needles will relate to plain and pattern stitches in the same way for tuck, slip, and lace, but may be reversed for fairisle and weave.

Choice of pattern and stitch

There are no rules about the type of pattern you should use for any particular stitch. Be adventurous, and be prepared to try anything once. However there are some things to avoid, simply because they are impractical.

The most obvious example is a fairisle design with large shapes, which cause long sagging floats on the reverse side. This would be a particular problem in sleeves for instance. There are several ways of dealing with this problem. The simplest is to limit the use of fairisle to small-scale designs. Large shapes may be broken up with an all-over texture, or scattered stitches of the contrast yarn. Floats may be stitched in on the reverse of the fabric after knitting. Iron-on interfacing may be applied to the reverse side, or the garment may be lined. If either of the two latter courses are taken, the elasticity of the knitting will be lost, and this will affect the style of garment for which it is suitable. Long vertical lines should be avoided in fairisle designs as the fabric tends to gape at the join of the two colours.

Tuck stitch should only be selected on one stitch at a time, as knitted stitches are needed on either side to hold the tucked yarn in place. Studio and Knitmaster tuck two consecutive stitches at once. If several needles together are selected to tuck, the yarn across them will tangle and jam on the following row. The same needle cannot be selected to tuck row after row. Periodically the tucked yarn must be knitted in. When knitting with 4 ply fingering, for example, the needle hook will be full after about six rows of tuck. If tucking is continued after this point, dropped loops will result. With a fine yarn, especially if knitting on selected needles only, twelve rows of tuck before knitting in may be possible.

Weights are important in knitting tuck patterns, to prevent the collected loops from jumping off the needle. They should be moved up frequently so that they are always pulling on the stitches that are knitting. Broad vertical stripes of plain and tuck should be avoided. Every time the carriage is passed across the needles, a row of stitches is produced in the plain area. But it takes several passes of the carriage to produce a row of stitches in the tuck area, as a proportion of the passes will produce tucks, not stitches. This means that the plain area is growing in length more rapidly than the tucked area. The result is a distorted and misshapen fabric. This method might be used deliberately to produce special effects such as gathering, by tucking up one edge on an otherwise plain fabric.

In slip stitch patterns there is the same limitation as in fairisle on the number of needles which may be selected together to slip, because of the danger of long floats catching. It is even more important in this case as the floats are on the face side. There is no practical limitation to the number of rows that slipping may be repeated on the same needles. However, if more than two or three rows are slipped without changing the needle selection, instead of producing the familiar float pattern, a rippled or pleated effect will result. Vertical stripes of slip and plain have the same disadvantages as in tuck stitch.

In lace patterns only single stitches may be select-ed as pattern stitches, i.e. there must be at least one plain stitch on either side of the pattern stitch. There must also be one row of plain before repeating a lace stitch on the same needle, or a ladder effect will result.

Weave patterns usually consist of a single stitch under which the laying in yarn is caught, alternating with one or more stitches over which it floats. The length of float possible without the danger of snagging depends on the thickness of the laying in yarn. The thicker it is, the longer the float possible.

It is not suggested that all designs are necessarily analysed in relation to the above points before they are tried on the machine. You will gradually learn to recognise at a glance the main things to avoid. If a pattern proves unsuccessful after one attempt on the machine, try to ascertain the reason, or use another stitch for which the design is perhaps more suitable.

Development of basic stitches

You should be completely confident in the use of the basic stitches on your machine before attempting some of the more adventurous methods suggested below as they do require a sound knowledge of the machine and how it works.

Fairisle

All machines are designed to knit two-colour fair-isle. In the case of non punch card machines how-ever, it is possible to knit more than two colours in a row. When knitting fairisle on these machines, needles knit yarn which has been laid across them by hand. It is possible therefore, to take several yarns across the needles before knitting each row, passing them on top of the needles where they are required to knit, and under the needles where they are required to float. It is important to make sure that every needle has some yarn on top of it before knitting the row, or a dropped stitch will result.

This technique is not possible on punch card machines as they will only knit yarn which is in one of the two feeders. The simplest way of getting multi-coloured fairisle effects on punch card machines is to combine fairisle with striping of the yarn in one or both feeders. By careful choice of pattern and stripes it is possible to lose the appearance of stripes altogether. Other methods of obtaining multi-coloured fairisle effects are by slip stitch combined with multi-coloured striping, and fairisle combined with short row knitting. Both these methods are described in later sections.

The wrong side of fairisle often gives an interesting design of floats in contrasting colours. A subtle type of pattern is achieved by knitting two yarns of the same colour but of a contrasting type and texture in a fairisle design. An all-over or small texture pattern is an alternative to the more normal method of knitting two yarns in one feeder, where a blend of colours is required. An extension of this idea is to use two yarns which will react differently to a finishing process: a mohair or angora yarn which will brush up into a furry pile, for example, combined with a smooth yarn, or a synthetic yarn combined with a natural yarn. When washed, one will shrink and the other will not, producing a blister effect. Using a shirring elastic or an elastomeric yarn combined with a conventional non-stretch yarn will produce a similar effect. If extremes of thick and thin yarn are used together, a looped pile effect will result on the reverse side. Needles out, i.e. knitting on selected needles only, can drastically alter a pattern, especially if it is on a small scale.

Tuck

Tuck stitch may be used to produce textures on either the face or reverse sides. Reverse side patterns are the most common. An all-over small scale pattern produces a honeycomb effect. More spaced out use of tuck stitches produces raised pattern areas. Remember that only one needle at a time will tuck, so large raised tuck areas are made by alternate tuck and plain stitches contrasted with areas of all plain. More bumpy textures are made by tucking several rows on the same needles before knitting in, e.g. by setting a pattern card to roll intermittently.

A fancy rib look may be made by patterns with strong vertical emphasis, but with short individual tucks. An example would be to set the pattern card on hold, but to change to plain knitting every third row. This rib effect may be emphasised when knitting with thick yarn by knitting with occasional needles out. Knitting on selected needles only in thin yarn will produce lace type patterns.

On the technical face side, undulating surfaces may be made by tucking over several rows on spaced out needles. This effect is exaggerated if tuck rows are knitted on a loose tension and plain rows on a tight tension. If this is reversed, with tuck rows tight and plain rows loose, a lace effect will result.

Colour patterns may be produced by combining tuck with striping. In contrast to fairisle there are no floats on the back. Here is a simple example of how it works. Two rows are knitted in black, knitting on even needles and tucking on odd needles. Then two rows are knitted white, knitting on odd needles and tucking on even needles. On the first two rows the black yarn only shows on the face side on even

stitches. On the second two rows the white yarn only shows on the face side on the odd stitches. So instead of a striped pattern, a spotted pattern shows on the face side. If this sequence is repeated an all-over spot or bird's eye pattern will result. A variation is to knit a row of tuck in black, alternated with rows of plain in white. On the face side, the black rows would be broken by white stitches, but the white rows would be unbroken, giving a pattern of isolated black stitches on a white ground.

On punch card machines any pattern card suitable for tuck will produce colour tuck patterns. The simplest way to use it is to put the card on hold, knit two or three rows of tuck in colour 1, then two or three rows of plain in colour 2. Then repeat. This will produce a checked pattern (fig. 40). This same

Figure 40 Stripes of tuck and plain, card on hold

Figure 41 Stripes of tuck and plain, card on release

method may be used with the card on release, the result depending on the particular card (fig. 41).

Tucking on all rows, with the card on release and combined with striping will produce a different pattern again. You must change colour on the same row that the needles selected to tuck change (fig. 42). On models with pre-selection of needles, this is easy to see as you go along, so it is not necessary to work out the striping beforehand.

There is a variation on the tuck stitch which is not limited, as the conventional method is, to selection of single pattern stitches. In fact there is no practical limit to the number of stitches together which may be selected. It is only possible to do it quickly on machines which have three positions for the holding cam levers. The use of the first two positions has been explained elsewhere. The third position has the effect, when a row is knitted, of bringing selected pattern needles to the full forward position, where they will stay until the lever is returned to position 'I'. On subsequent rows therefore, the yarn will not knit on these needles but just be laid across them.

When the lever is returned to position 'I', the selected needles will knit back in, catching in the floats from the previous rows. Because the tucked yarn is not held in the hook of the needle, many more rows may be tucked before it is necessary to knit them in. Similar colour and lace patterns as in conventional tuck are possible.

Slip

Slip stitch is normally used for all-over float patterns on the reverse side of the fabric. A raised effect is made by knitting areas of slip pattern surrounded by large areas of plain. If the same needles are selected to slip repeatedly over several rows (e.g. with the pattern card on hold), followed by a row or two of plain, a pronounced ripple effect will result. This may be used decoratively, or to produce light bulky fabric with good insulating properties.

If this same method of slipping repeatedly on the same needles, followed by a row of plain, is used with one needle knitting alternating with several needles

1 Intarsia technique used to make a multi-coloured geometric design

2 Slip stitch used to make an undulating surface and to distort stripes

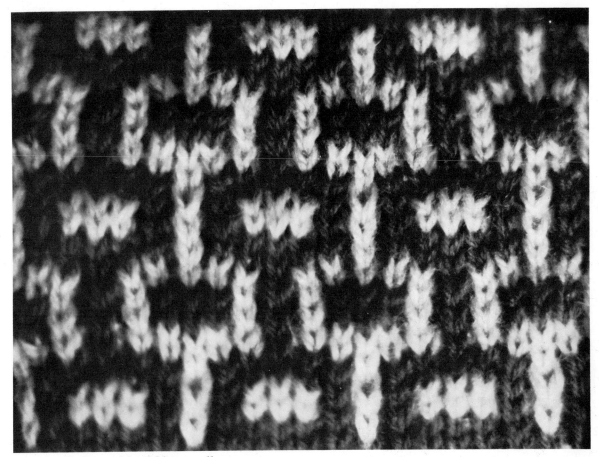

Figure 42 Stripes with tucking on all rows

slipping, a thick loop pile fabric will result. Slip stitch may also be used as an alternative to weaving, for inlaying thick or difficult yarns, particularly on older models without weaving brushes. Several rows of plain in the basic yarn are followed by one row of slip in the fancy yarn. The needle selection for this row should be one needle knitting alternating with several needles slipping.

Slip stitch combined with striping may also be used to produce colour patterns, on the technical face side. It is a useful technique on older machines which are not equipped to knit fairisle, and may also be used on punch card machines to produce fairisle patterns with more than two colours in a row. The principle is the same as for making colour patterns in tuck stitch. Two rows of slip stitch are knitted in colour 1. Then needles selected for knitting and slipping are reversed and two rows of slip are knitted in colour 2. Always select the first needle in the row to knit, regardless of the pattern, to ensure that each yarn floats right to the edge of the fabric. The colours will only show through to the face side on the

stitches that were knitted in their rows, so four passes of the carriage are necessary to make two rows of finished knitting.

For three-colour fairisle the procedure is as follows. Select needles required to knit colour 1. Set the carriage to slip stitch. Knit two rows in colour 1. Select the needles required to knit colour 2. Knit two rows in colour 2. Select the needles required to knit colour 3. Knit two rows of colour 3. Two rows of the pattern have now been completed, although the carriage has been passed across the needles six times. This is a slow process, only suitable for areas of detail or borders, especially since on punch card machines no ready-made cards would be suitable, and needles might have to be selected by hand. Punch cards may however be adapted to this purpose by taping over the holes with cellophane tape. This technique is described in detail in a later section. An alternative way of using slip stitch to knit multi-coloured fairisle is to select the stitches for colour 1, knit one row, then knit in other colours one at a time by hand as described on page 33.

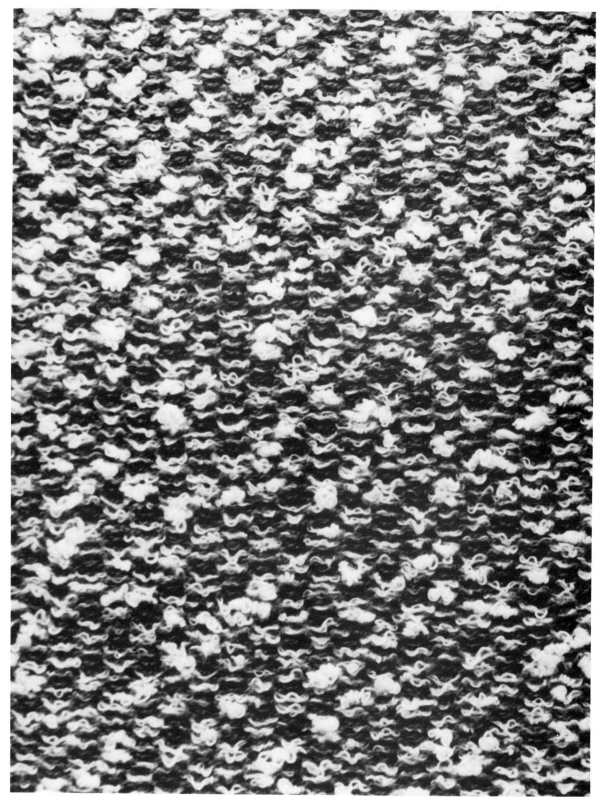

Figure 43 Weave with textured inlay yarn

Weave

Weaving fabrics are usually used on the reverse side to make the most of the inlay yarn. The face side may also be used for more subtle effects, as the inlay yarn shows through slightly, especially if the same pattern needles are selected for several consecutive rows. Knitting with occasional needles out will also help to show the inlay yarn more on the face side. Using a high proportion of needles out and fine yarn will produce a lacy fabric.

The inlay yarn has the same effect as when using tuck stitch for lacy fabrics; it gives an otherwise flimsy fabric a certain stability. It is normally recommended that the inlay yarn is relatively thick, but delicate effects may be achieved with fine inlay yarns and thick knitting yarn, especially if the inlay yarn is textured (fig. 43). Floats of fine yarn should be only one needle wide because of the danger of snagging.

Weave patterns normally consist of a single pattern needle which knits over the weaving yarn, alternating with two or three needles over which it floats. As a variation two or more pattern needles may be selected together, in which case the weaving yarn only weaves under half a stitch at a time, producing an undulating line, instead of the straight inlay of the normal method. Long floats may be knitted and then cut through to produce tufts.

Vertical inlay is a way of making designs with long verticals in them, which is difficult in other patterning methods. It is not possible to produce vertical inlay on Knitmasters because they do not have pre-selection of needles. Here is an example of how it works. Alternate needles are brought to the forward pattern position. On punch card machines this is done by inserting the number one card, engaging the needles to the pattern card and knitting one row in plain.

Lay two different yarns across two pattern needles at different points. With the weaving brushes in place knit one row. Each yarn will weave into the stitches of the needles they were laid across. Lay each yarn back across the same needles. Knit one row. As the knitting progresses the two weaving yarns will make zigzag vertical lines. The pattern needle selection and width of stripes may be varied to give a wide choice of effects.

Lace

The lace carriage performs the same task as the transfer tool, but it transfers a whole row of selected stitches in one movement. It is not necessary to set up the needle bed extensions provided with lace carriage machines just to do samples and narrow pieces. The lace carriage may be passed in either direction regardless of the direction of the knitting. Any stitch transfer pattern may be knitted on a machine without a lace carriage by transfer tool, but this would take much longer. It would only be practical for details, such as borders.

The lace carriage on Brother punch card machines may be adjusted to make 'fine lace'. It then transfers a stitch to the next needle but without the stitch being dropped from the original needle. Thus the one stitch is stretched across both needles. This may also be done by transfer tool on other machines.

Needles may be pushed back to the non-knitting position after stitches have been transferred off, and then brought back into knitting after several rows for ladder effects as described on page 42. Larger holes and a cable effect are possible when knitting on selected needles only. The stitch selected should have an empty needle on one side and a knitting needle on the other. It must of course be transferred in the direction of the knitting needle.

Stitch transfer may be used to produce a raised stitch pattern by changing to a looser tension on pattern rows. Here is an example. Knit several rows of plain on a tight tension. Knit one row on a loose tension, selecting alternate needles. Transfer the stitches. Change back to tight tension and knit several rows of plain. Decorative ribbon and cord may be added by threading them in and out of the rows of lace holes. Most lace patterns combine stitches transferred to left and to right. If stitches are constantly transferred in the same direction, a pronounced diagonal grain, and even a diagonally shaped fabric, will result.

Interesting patterns are achieved by making several transfers of stitches between each row of knitting. It is possible to transfer to left and to right in the same row or to transfer several adjacent stitches one at a time, each moving on to a needle left empty by the one before. These types of pattern are relatively easy to do on non punch card machines with independent needle selection.

They are also particularly easy, with the right pattern card, on the Brother punch card machine, because the lace carriage incorporates its own needle selector. On the Toyota, Singer and Juki, needle selection depends on a pass of the knitting carriage. It is possible to make a needle selection without knitting, by passing the carriage, set to slip. It is simpler on these machines though to make needle selections by hand if more than one transfer per row of knitting is required.

Lace knitting on Knitmaster and Studio punch

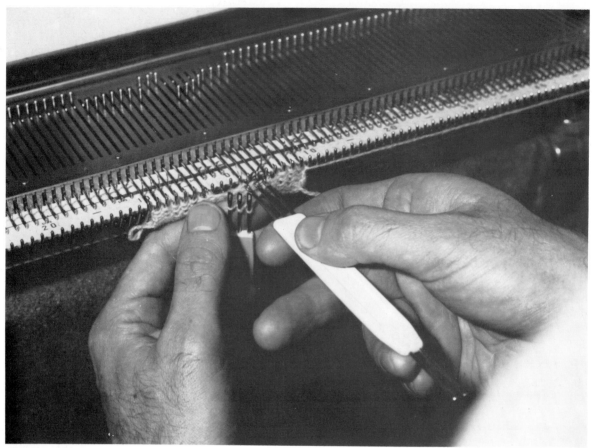

Figure 44 Making cable

card machines is not based on stitch transfer at all. A thick and a thin yarn are knitted together and on pattern stitches the thick yarn is slipped while the thin yarn knits, giving a lacy effect. A transparent filament yarn is recommended for the thin yarn by Knitmaster, to give the illusion of a hole on the pattern stitches, but this adversely affects the handle of the fabric because of its harshness. Any fine yarn in a matching colour will give a lacy effect. Overlocking cotton, because it is very fine and comes on cones ready to knit, is particularly suitable. Decorative fine yarns such as metallics may also be used. If knitted on a tight tension, Knitmaster lace will give a solid fabric with a slip stitch look but a softer handle.

Hand techniques

Lace stitch and tucking by use of the transfer tool have already been described. To make cable, two three-stitch transfer tools are required. Every few rows, two adjacent groups of three stitches are swopped over on the needle bed. The following procedure will simplify the problem of handling two transfer tools at once.

Transfer the right-hand group of stitches to the tool. Transfer the tool to the left-hand and hold. Transfer the left-hand group of stitches to the second tool, and thence to the empty right-hand needles. Take the tool holding the remaining stitches in the right-hand and transfer to the empty left-hand needles (fig. 44). Reverse the use of the right and left hands if you are left-handed. It is important always to replace the stitches back on the needles in the same order (in the example given, onto the right-hand needles first).

The knitting tension needs to be relatively loose for the thickness of yarn because the stitches have to be stretched so much. Weights are needed beneath where the cable is being made to help smooth the transfer of stitches. The number of rows between each transfer is according to choice and will affect the finished appearance. A minimum of three rows is required before the stitches will stretch enough to make the cross. Large cables, as seen in hand or rib

Figure 45 Lattice stitch

knitting, are not possible, although several cables may be made side by side.

A variation on cable which may be extended over a large area is lattice stitch. Transfer tools with two eyes are needed. Here is an example worked over twelve needles. Knit five rows plain. Swop the first left-hand pair of stitches with the second pair, transferring the stitches onto the right-hand needles first. Swop pair three with pair four, transferring the stitches onto the right-hand needles first. Swop pair five with pair six, transferring the stitches onto the right-hand needles first. Knit five rows. Ignore pair one on the left. Swop pair two with pair three, transferring the stitches onto the *left-hand* needles first. Swop pair four with pair five, transferring the stitches onto the left-hand needles first. Repeat from the beginning. See figure 45 for an example of lattice stitch.

Purl stitch patterns are made in a similar way to latch hook ribbing. With some knitting already on the machine, drop a stitch, and ladder it back several rows. Insert the latch hook from the reverse side (i.e. from the side facing you) into the first unladdered stitch and re-knit the laddered stitch back up to the top. Replace the top stitch onto the needle. Purl stitches may be used individually or in groups to make whole shapes of purl stitch. How far back the dropped stitch ladders may be controlled by holding the knitting with the thumb firmly against the stitch where the ladder should stop, or by hooking the latch hook into the appropriate stitch before the ladder is made. If all stitches are to be laddered down to the same row, a length of yarn may be temporarily threaded into this row as a stopper.

Fringes or tufts may be knitted in. Ideally you should have a casting on comb for this job. With several rows already knitted, select alternate needles. Hold the casting on comb about 5cm (2 inches) below the needle bed with the hooks towards you. Take the yarn for the fringe over the first selected needle, inside the hook, and under the corresponding hook on the comb. Continue over and under across the whole width. Knit one row. The fringe yarn will knit in with the main yarn on alternate needles. It will be held more firmly in the fabric if it is wound round the needle hook one complete turn before taking it down and under the hook on the comb.

The importance of the comb, besides gauging the length of the loops, is that it holds the yarn firmly in the hook while the stitch is made. If the fringe is to be only four or five needles wide it is possible to hold the loops down firmly by hand while the row is knitted. If several rows of fringe are to be knitted, the comb should be hung below the needle bed at the appropriate height.

Swiss darning, which is done after the knitting has been removed from the machine, is really a form of embroidery particularly suited to knitted fabrics. It is also used to correct mistakes in fairisle patterns and is described in detail in the chapter 'Common Problems'.

Combining stitches

The simplest way of combining different pattern stitches in one piece of knitting is in stripes. On some machines it is possible to select one stitch for knitting from right to left and another for rows knitted from left to right. On other machines it would involve a flick of a switch on the carriage. The result may be quite different from either of the original stitches.

It is possible in some cases to combine two different stitches in the same row, which almost amounts to making a new type of stitch. Tuck stitch may be combined with any other stitch simply by making pick up tucks with the transfer tool as described on page 42, after each row of patterning.

Tucks using the holding position method may also be combined with any other pattern stitch. Here is an example of how to do it combined with slip stitch. Select every fourth needle to knit. Bring every other knit needle (every eighth needle) to the forward hold position. Set the carriage to slip. Set the holding cam control to hold. Knit four rows. The yarn will knit on every eighth needle and the long floats will tuck over the hold position needles. Set the carriage to plain and the holding cam control to knit in. Knit one row. There are many variations of pattern and stitch which may be combined with use of the holding cams in this way.

Stitch transfer lace may be combined with any other stitch in the same row. The simplest method, as with tuck, is to use the transfer tool to make lace holes after each row of pattern knitting. Another way on non punch card machines is to make a needle selection, transfer stitches with the lace carriage, and make a second needle selection. Knit one pattern row. On punch card machines, pattern card and lace carriage may be used in the normal way. Then a second needle selection is made by hand and a pattern row is knitted. The Brother lace carriage will transfer stitches and make a second needle selection, according to the pattern card, in one movement.

Designing on the machine

The best way to work out new texture and stitch ideas is by trial and error on the machine. Only with a great deal of experience is it possible to forecast the effect of combining various yarns and stitches, and even then not with any certainty. To a lesser extent this is true of colour combinations too, although it is possible to twist yarns or group balls of yarn together to get some idea before knitting a sample.

This approach may result in some total failures and some designs which are just not suitable for the job in hand, but the time spent doing them has not necessarily been wasted. Samples should be kept in a note book with details of how they were done, especially what stitch tension was used. This is the easiest thing to forget, and the most difficult to work out later. This note book may well provide you with just the pattern you want at some future date and will probably suggest new ideas to follow as well.

With the exception of the Knitmaster punch card models, it is possible to select pattern needles by hand, and this is the most immediate way of trying out a new stitch idea, and may later be transposed to a punch card if it is successful. The various non punch card machines are all operated row by row, so it is not necessary to work out a pattern before the sample is knitted. It can be made up as you go along, and then a note can be made of the sequence of pattern rows.

A lot of original designs may be made on punch card machines without punching out a new pattern, by knitting rows in contrasting pattern stitches as already described. Patterns may be elongated by knitting each pattern row twice. On machines which do not have a setting to do this, it is done by knitting one row with the card on hold and one row with the card on release. A distorting mirror effect is made by gradually increasing and decreasing the number of rows knitted on hold. The card may be kept permanently on hold. When knitting slip or tuck on hold, rows of plain must be introduced. Completely new designs will result from rolling the card back and forth by hand to selected rows on the pattern.

Punch card and hand selection methods may be combined by, for example, altering every other repeat by hand before knitting each row. Cards may be altered temporarily by taping over selected holes with cellophane tape, or permanently by punching extra holes. Two cards may be fed into the machine together, leaving holes only where they coincide in the two patterns. Cards may be cut up into short sections and clipped together in a different order, with some sections upside down, or back to front, or sections from several different cards might be combined.

Designing on paper

Some designs, especially those with large repeats, will have to be worked out on paper before a sample may be knitted. It is not worth doing more than a rough sketch before drawing out the stitch plan on squared paper, as the original idea may have to be adjusted and revised before it will fit the squares and the repeats match up properly. The procedure is the same for punch card and non punch card machines. Patterns drawn on squared paper will appear longer in proportion than when knitted. This is because the paper has the same number of rows and stitches in a square area, whereas knitting will always have more rows than stitches. Sometimes sheets of design paper are supplied with blank cards which are divided in the correct proportions for the drawing to match the knitting.

First of all the stitch repeat size must be decided. For punch card machines this will normally be 24 stitches but a fraction of 24 may be used, i.e. 12, 8, 4, 3 or 2. Stitch repeat size on other machines will depend on the model. The length of the repeat may be any number of rows you choose. Blank pattern cards are sixty rows long, but they may be lengthened or shortened as appropriate. As an example we will take a pattern 24 stitches by 40 rows.

Draw a rectangle 24 squares wide by 40 squares long in the middle of the graph paper, extending the lines well beyond the corners where they cross. Lightly sketch the design in the rectangle. Fill in appropriate squares or outline large shapes and at the same time fill in half a repeat all round the rectangle. For example, if a square at the left of the rectangle is filled in, the corresponding square in the next repeat to the right should be filled in. If a square in the bottom right-hand corner is filled in, the corresponding squares in the repeats to the left, above, and in the corner diagonally opposite should be filled in (fig. 46). This will show if the repeats are matching up as they should and how they will look as an all-over pattern. This is a much better method

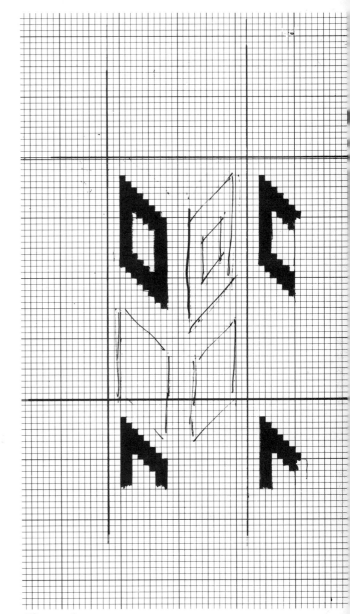

Figure 46

than completing the whole design before filling in the repeats.

As the squares relate only approximately to the original line drawing, the design may be drastically changed in the squaring up process, especially if it includes curved outlines or if it is a figurative design. Stand back from the drawing and squint slightly to make the squares disappear and to get a stronger impression of the shapes. The outlines may be improved by altering individual squares. Even so, final alterations may have to be made after a sample has been knitted. The change from squares to stitches may have a similar distorting effect as from line drawing to squared design. Once the graphed design has been finalised, either a card must be punched, or on non punch card machines a sample may be knitted directly by following the drawing row by row.

To avoid making mistakes in punching, the card should be marked square by square first, except for very simple geometric designs. The whole area of a pattern card must be punched. If a design with a repeat of 12 stitches by 20 rows has been drawn, it must be repeated twice across and three times down the card when punching it out. A quicker way would be to repeat it twice across and only twice down and cut the remainder off.

Two extra rows at the bottom of the second repeat must be included. These two rows are punched all holes for the overlap. Punch two holes either side matched with the top end to take the clips, and cut a little off the width next to these holes, again to match the top end, otherwise the clips will not fit on without bending the card. Cards should not be cut down to less than about forty rows or they will not be long enough to join round into a continuous pattern.

The stitch that the pattern is intended for must be borne in mind. As we have already seen, not all patterns are suitable for all stitches. As a broad rule, cards with large areas of holes, but no large areas of blanks, are suitable for tuck and slip. Cards with large areas of blanks, but no large areas of holes, are suitable for lace. Cards with no large areas at all are suitable for weave. Cards with large areas of holes and large areas blanks are suitable for fairisle.

The square, block repeat effect of patterns may be avoided by off-setting repeated shapes down the card, and by drawing lines and shapes across the edge of the repeat (fig. 47).

Traditional-look designs might be based on embroidery and woven fabrics as well as traditional knitwear. They can only be used as a starting point and must be adapted to the limitations and capabilities of the particular machine.

Colour

Most yarns come in a limited range of standard colours, with only enough shades for designs of strong contrasts and bold effects. There are not the intermediate tones needed for more subtle colour harmonies. One way round this problem is to buy yarns of similar quality from several different suppliers, so that several slightly different shades of each basic colour may be obtained. A bright colour may be toned down to obtain a more original colour effect by combining it with a more neutral shade in an all-over fairisle or weave pattern.

Buying a quantity of white or natural yarn and dyeing the colours yourself is the answer, if you have the time. Left-over yarns in unwanted colours may be tinted by over-dyeing with a weak solution of dye. If a strong dye solution of a contrasting colour is used, it will result in a dark drab shade. Once you have launched into the business of dyeing your own colours, all the possibilities of multi-coloured yarns are open to you with techniques such as tie and dip dyeing. Methods and techniques of dyeing are beyond the scope of this book but information is available from dye suppliers and from specialist publications.

Figure 47

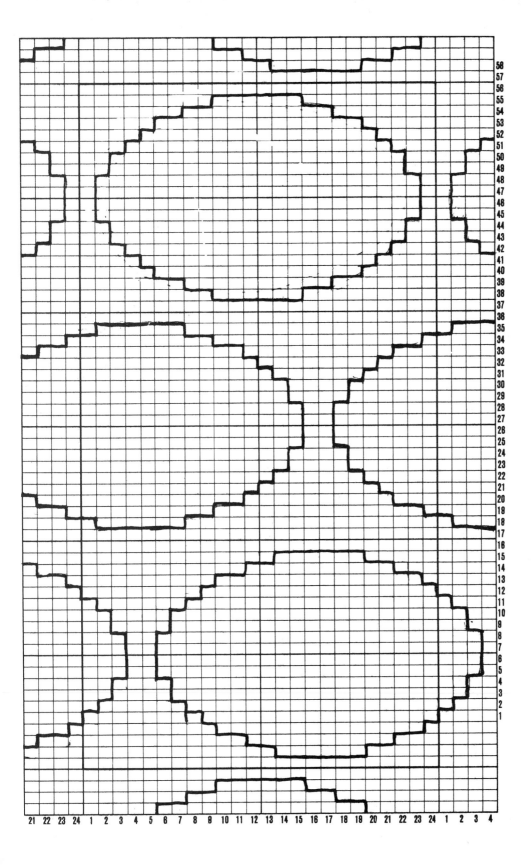

58
57
56
55
54
53
52
51
50
49
48
47
46
45
44
43
42
41
40
39
38
37
36
35
34
33
32
31
30
29
28
27
26
25
24
23
22
21
20
19
18
17
16
15
14
13
12
11
10
9
8
7
6
5
4
3
2
1

21 22 23 24 1 2 3 4 5 6 7 8 9 10 11 12 13 14 15 16 17 18 19 20 21 22 23 24 1 2 3 4

Advanced Designs

Special techniques are required for making large scale and three-dimensional designs. One way of making a non-repeating design across the whole width of the machine has already been mentioned, i.e. to hand select pattern needles at the beginning of each row. This method is not possible on Knitmaster punch card machines, and on all machines it is a very slow process. There are, however, other ways of making designs bigger than the normal repeat size.

Partial patterning

Method

Select pattern either by feeding in a card pattern or by another method. Set the holding cam control to knit in. Bring all the needles required to knit plain to the forward position. Knit one row. The forward needles will knit back to the normal knitting position, but in plain knitting; the other needles will knit the pattern. Continue, bringing the needles required to knit plain to the forward position at the beginning of each row.

In fairisle partial patterning, the forward needles will be knitted in colour 2. On pre-select machines, needles may also be selected to knit plain in colour 1 by bringing them back to the normal knitting position 'B'. It is therefore possible to have plain areas in both colours knitting in the same row. When isolated areas of pattern or borders are knitted by the forward needle method, it is necessary to prevent yarn 1 from making a float right to the edge of the knitting. This is done by bringing this yarn under the first forward needle next to the pattern area, but over the rest of the forward needles at the end of each row (fig. 48).

For stitch transfer lace the needles required to knit plain should be returned to 'B' position before passing the lace carriage across. The manual method of partial patterning described here is not suitable for Knitmaster lace.

For partial weave patterning on pre-selection machines, needles required to knit plain should be returned to the 'B' position before knitting each row. The manual method of partial patterning is not suitable for weaving on Knitmaster machines.

Besides the manual methods already described, the latest models from Toyota and Knitmaster have mechanical aids to make partial patterning quicker and easier. However, in both cases their use is limited. On Knitmaster 323 machines, a metal plate 24 stitches wide is placed on the needle bed behind the needles required to knit pattern, and extra cams are attached to the carriage. It is not possible by this method to select less than 24 stitches at a time to knit pattern. On Knitmaster 326 machines, clips are placed behind the needles at the left-hand side, and at the right-hand side of the section to knit pattern. Pattern sections of any width may be knitted by this method. Both methods may be used with lace, weave or fairisle, but not with tuck or slip stitch patterns, nor with any yarn requiring a tension looser than 7.

On the Toyota 787, any single repeat across the bed may be selected to knit pattern with the remainder knitting plain, simply by turning a knob. It may be used with fairisle, weave, and lace, but not with slip or tuck. For selective slip or tuck patterns, or for more than one pattern repeat in a row, the manual method must be used.

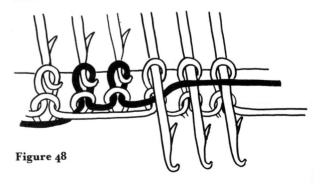

Figure 48

58

Figure 49

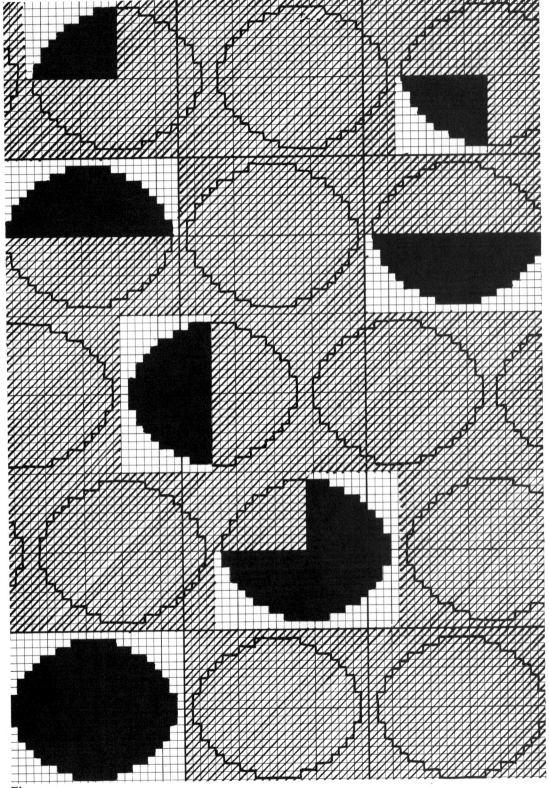

Figure 50

Uses

Figure 49 shows, in diagramatic form, the effect of spacing out a simple all-over stitch pattern by selecting alternate areas to knit plain. The shaded stitches are selected to knit plain and the unshaded stitches knit according to the pattern. The pattern stitches that will show in the fabric are depicted in solid black, giving a checked pattern twice the normal repeat size. This pattern is most suitable for tuck or slip stitch. If it was knitted in fairisle the long floats that would result would have to be dealt with by one of the methods already described.

Figure 50 shows how different shapes are knitted from the same pattern card. The pattern shown in figure 47 is used as an example. Again the shaded stitches are selected to knit plain, and the unshaded stitches knit according to the pattern. The solid black shapes are the ones that will show in the knitting. This pattern would be suitable to knit in fairisle. As only one shape is selected to knit at a time there is no problem with long floats.

Figure 51 shows how an image wider than the normal maximum of 24 stitches may be achieved by partial patterning. The 24-stitch-wide pattern depicts the back wheel, hood and driver of an old fashioned touring car. For sixteen rows, 40 stitches are selected to knit pattern. The 13 stitches on the left include the wheel and back panel of the car in front, which become the front wheel and bonnet of our car. The 3 stitches on the right include the front panel of the car behind which becomes the boot of our car. For the remaining 12 rows, 25 stitches are

selected to knit pattern. One stitch on the left includes the back of the hood of the car in front, which becomes the windscreen of our car. This method may be used to create large images of other subjects which have a certain element of repetition such as trees in a landscape, windows in a building, carriages in a train, and so on.

As we have seen, fairisle is best suited to single image or border patterning. Small areas of plain may be knitted in the middle of a pattern area, but if a wide section of plain is knitted, there is the problem of long floats. Conversely tuck and slip are best suited to alternate spaced patterns, because of the problem of distortion and puckering with border or vertical stripe patterns in these stitches. Stitch transfer lace is suitable for all types of partial patterning. Weaving is best suited to borders and single images again because of the problem of floats, in this case on the face side. On pre-select machines (i.e. all machines except Knitmaster punch card models) there is a quicker and more versatile method of obtaining selective weave patterns which is described in a later section.

Intarsia

Intarsia is a method of colour patterning in which each yarn knits back and forth within its own shape instead of floating at the back when not required in the pattern, as in fairisle. There is no limit to the number of colours that may be knitted in one row, and because of the lack of floats it is possible to knit

Figure 51

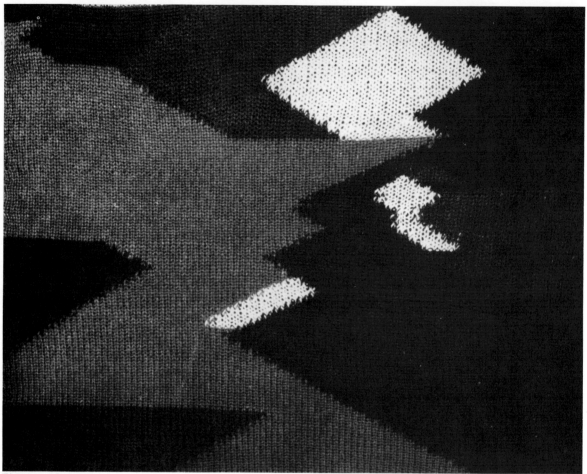

Figure 52 Intarsia

large shapes (fig. 52). Intarsia is only possible on simpler machines which do not have a second feeder on the sinker plate for fairisle knitting. It is not possible on punch card machines.

The machine is set up as if to knit fairisle. All needles are brought to the position for knitting the pattern colour, usually position 'C'. A ball of yarn is required for each shape. So if a black shape is to be knitted against a white background, one ball of white for the left side, one ball of black for the centre shape, and one ball of white for the right-hand side is required. Place the balls of yarn on the floor in front of the machine. Lay an end of yarn in the appropriate colour across each group of needles, with the short end on the side nearest the carriage, and overlapping each colour with its neighbour by one needle (fig. 53).

Pass the empty carriage across, so knitting each colour in on its appropriate needles. Bring the needles back to position 'C' (if this is not done

automatically). Lay the yarns back across the needles in the same way. Knit one row and continue. Designs may be drawn out on graph paper first, or irregular patterns may be made up as you go along.

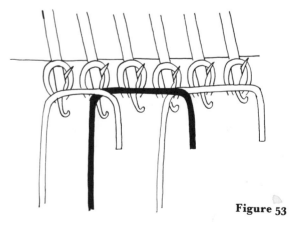

Figure 53

Multi-coloured inlay

This patterning method is based on weaving, and may be used on pre-select machines fitted with weave brushes. Select the pattern needles. Any pattern may be used, but a small all-over pattern is most suitable. Set the weaving brushes to the operational position. As for intarsia, a ball of yarn is required for each separate shape, plus an extra yarn for knitting which is threaded through the tensioner and into the yarn feed in the normal way.

Place the balls on the floor before the machine. Lay the end of the appropriate yarn across each group of needles with the short end nearest the carriage. The yarn will rest on selected needles only. It is not necessary to overlap the yarns, although overlapping by one needle will give a stronger, more stable fabric. Not overlapping will give more definite outlines to the shapes.

With the yarn in the feeder, knit one row. Each pattern yarn will weave into the knitting on its respective needles. Select the needles and lay the yarn back across them in the opposite direction. Knit one row and continue. The background yarn chosen to knit with will show on the surface, even if it is very fine in relation to inlay yarns. The colour of the knitting must be chosen carefully, therefore,

not to clash with any of the pattern colours. If a wide range of pattern colours is being used, a neutral knitting yarn is generally best.

This method of knitting works best with the machine set back at an angle. If your machine is normally used flat it might be worthwhile getting an extra pair of angled clamps. Figure 54 shows an example of multi-coloured inlay combined with striping.

Short row patterning

The effect of short row patterning is identical to intarsia, except that vertical joins are not practical, so designs must be based on diagonal and horizontal lines. However, short row patterning is possible on all types of machine. Here is an example of how to knit a diagonal join between two colours.

Thread colour 1. Cast on 20 stitches and knit several rows in plain. Finish with the carriage on the left. Set the holding cam control to hold. Bring the first right-hand needle to the forward position. Knit one row. Take the yarn under the first needle. Knit one row. Bring the second right-hand needle to the forward position. Knit one row. Take the yarn under the second forward needle and over the first. Knit

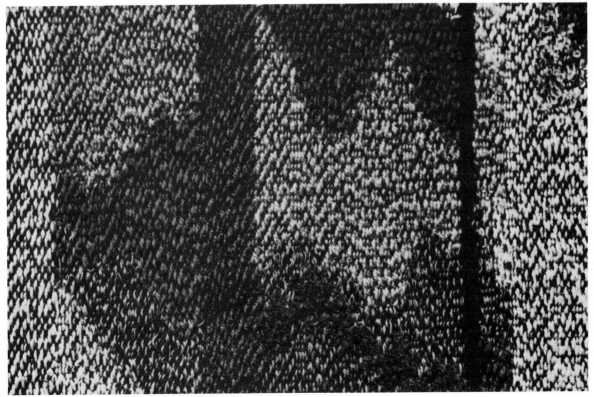

Figure 54 Multi-coloured inlay and striping

one row. Continue knitting, bringing one needle forward before knitting to the right, and always taking the yarn under this needle before knitting to the left, as in figure 48. If the yarn is not taken under the needle, lace stitches will form an outline to the shape.

Stop when there is only one needle on the left still knitting. Remove the yarn from the feeder. Bring the last needle on the left to the forward position. Take the empty carriage across to the left-hand side. The needles will not move. Thread colour 2. Using the transfer tool, return the first right-hand needle to the knitting position. Knit two rows. Bring the second right-hand needle to the knitting position. Knit two rows. Continue until only one needle on the left is in the hold position.

A weight should always be hung immediately below the edge of the section actually knitting. This means that the weight must be continually moved in and out as the knitting progresses. An alternative, which is quicker with practice, is to pull down by hand at the right place as each row is knitted. If this is not done the edge stitch will drop off its needle. Also, with practice, use of the transfer tool may be dispensed with. Forward needles may simply be pushed back far enough so that they knit, but not so far that the stitches fall off.

The angle of join may be varied by bringing two or more needles out at a time. However, if four rows are knitted in between bringing out each needle, to get a steeper angle, there will be large holes at the join. It is impossible to get a solid edge at a steep angle. Short row patterning may be used in conjunction with any type of pattern knitting, with striping, or with any combination of pattern stitches as well as with plain knitting.

Three-dimensional effects

Short row patterning may also be used to knit folds and bumps. Here are two examples. Cast on 25 stitches. Knit several rows, and finish with the carriage on the right. Set the holding cam control on hold. Bring the first 10 needles on the left to the forward position. Knit one row. Bring 10 right-hand needles to the forward position. Knit one row. Make sure the weights are pulling on the centre section. Knit five rows. Using the transfer tool, return the forward needles on the right to the knitting position. Knit one row. Set the holding cam control to knit in position. Knit one row. You will now have knitted a fold.

Cast on 30 stitches. Knit several rows. Finish with the carriage on the right. Set the holding cam con-

trol on hold. Bring 10 left-hand needles to the forward position. Knit one row. Bring 10 right-hand needles to the forward position. Knit one row. Bring the next needle on the left to the forward position. Knit one row. Bring the next needle on the right to the forward position. Continue until there are only two needles knitting and the carriage is on the right. Using the transfer tool, return the left-hand needles to the knitting position. Knit one row. Set the holding cam control to knit in. Knit one row. You have knitted a bump. Figure 55 shows an example of short row used both three-dimensionally and to combine varied colours and textures of yarn.

Points, flaps and floating panels may be knitted in. Before starting the main knitting, knit panels to any shape or design, finishing on waste yarn. Cast on, and start the main knitting. At the row where the panel is to be joined, pick up the top row of stitches of the panel onto the needles, and unravel the waste. Continue knitting.

Gathers may be knitted by the short row method too. Here is an example. Cast on 30 stitches, with the carriage on the right. Knit two rows. Set the holding cam control on hold. Bring 10 left-hand needles to the forward position. Knit two rows. Bring the 11th needle to the forward position. Knit two rows. Continue until 15 needles are in the forward position. Knit two rows. Return the 15th needle to the knitting position. Knit two rows. Return the 14th needle to the knitting position. Continue until only 10 needles remain in the forward position. Set the holding cam control to knit in. Repeat from the beginning. It is especially important to take the yarn under the first forward needle before knitting from left to right. If the needles are held on the left and right sides, the centre section will form into swags or puckers depending on size.

Figure 55 Short row patterning

Shaping

Increasing

Simple increasing is only possible on one side at a time (i.e. on the same side as the carriage). To increase one stitch, bring the next empty needle to the forward position with the holding cam control at the knit in position. If the holding cam control is required to be at the hold position because of the pattern being knitted, bring the empty needle only to knitting position 'B'. A firmer edge is made by wrapping the yarn round the empty needle as in casting on, before knitting the row. To increase by more than one stitch at a time, bring the number of needles required to the forward position, and wrap the yarn round each one in turn, as in casting on.

Decreasing

A single stitch decrease may be made on both sides at once. Using the transfer tool, transfer the edge stitch in one needle, and return the emptied needle to the non-knitting position, so that the edge needle now has two stitches on it. This method of decreasing, although the quickest, sometimes makes too tight an edge. To make a looser edge, knit the two stitches in by hand as in casting off, before knitting the next row. This may only be done on the same side as the carriage. To decrease by more than one stitch at a time, cast off the required number on the side of the knitting nearest the carriage.

Fully fashioned shaping

This makes a decorative feature of seams as often seen on raglan shoulders. A triple transfer tool is used. To decrease, pick up the three edge stitches on the transfer tool, and transfer them all in by one needle (fig. 56).

To increase, pick up the three edge stitches and move them all out by one needle. Pick up a stitch from the row below onto the empty needle (fig. 57).

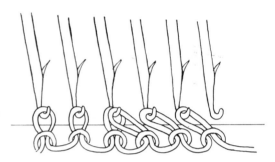

Figure 56

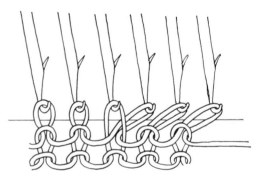

Figure 57

Fully fashioned shaping may be made on either side of the knitting. A more pronounced effect is made by transferring six stitches, three at a time, starting with the inside stitches for decreasing and with the outside stitches for increasing. Two stitches may be decreased in a row by moving the three stitches all two needles inwards.

Decreasing by holding stitches

This is a quick method of decreasing at shallow angles, (e.g. shoulders), especially if the piece is to be finished on waste yarn and not cast off. Decrease on the opposite side to the carriage. Set the holding cam control to hold. Bring the number of needles required to decrease to the forward position. Continue knitting and bringing the needles to the forward position every second row, until the shaping is finished. On the last row, slide the carriage clear of both the knitting and the holding needles.

To finish on the waste yarn, cut the knitting yarn and pull the end down below the needles. Thread a contrasting yarn. Set the holding cam control to knit in. Knit several rows and remove the knitting from the needles.

To cast off with shaping on one side only, finish with the carriage on the side opposite the holding needles, and cast off all stitches in the normal way, whether they are on the knitting or holding needles.

To cast off with shaping on both sides, cut the yarn and pull it down below the needles. Retain the main knitting yarn in the feeder, and tie off the end below the table to the left of the knitting. Cast off from left to right with the knitting yarn in the normal way.

Divided shapes

Knit divided shapes, e.g. 'V' necks, as follows. Set the holding cam control on hold. With the carriage on the right, bring all the needles left of the centre to the forward position. Shape the right side, making sure that the weights are pulling on the section actually being knitted, as described for short row knitting (page 64). Cast off the right side. Set the holding cam control to knit in. Tie the end of the knitting yarn to the clamp. Shape the left side. When knitting pattern stitches, note at which row the division was made, and be sure to feed in this pattern row before beginning the second side.

Horizontal darts

Here is an example of how to knit horizontal darts, e.g. bust darts. Set the holding cam control on hold. With the carriage on the right, bring two left-hand needles to the forward position. Knit two rows. Bring two more needles on the left to the forward position. Knit two rows. Continue until 10 needles are in the forward position and the carriage is at the right. Set the holding cam control to knit in. Continue knitting. This has made a dart 10 stitches wide by 10 rows deep. The depth may be varied by changing the number of rows knitted, and the proportionate width may be varied by changing the number of needles brought forward at a time.

The knitting can be made to turn a corner, as in sock heels for example, by making a dart virtually

Figure 58

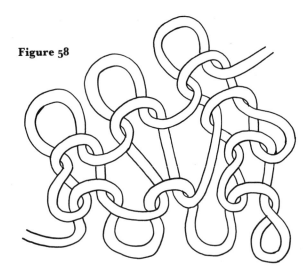

the whole width of the knitting (fig. 58). A series of such darts will make a curved shape, e.g. a flared skirt. To get a level hem, the individual sections must be symmetrical. Bring the needles to the forward position in the way already described, four needles every row, until four or less needles are knitting. Leave the holding cam control on hold, and return the needles to knitting in reverse order, four needles every other row. Figure 59 shows an example of a skirt made by this method in space-dyed yarn.

Figure 59 Skirt in space-dyed yarn, designed by Melissa Warren

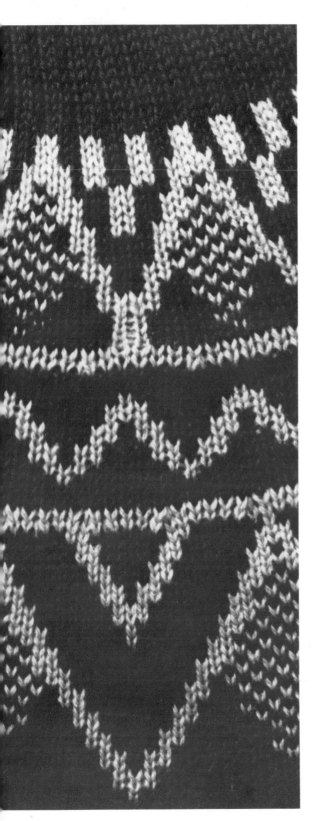

Vertical darts

Here is an example of how to knit a vertical dart, e.g. a waist dart in a straight skirt. Cast on 21 stitches and knit a few rows. Transfer the centre stitch onto the next needle to the left. Using the triple transfer tool, move the next three stitches on the right one needle to the left. Carry on transferring stitches across to the left until the right-hand needle is empty. Push the right-hand needle to the non-knitting position. Continue knitting for 20 rows, repeating the transferring process every fourth row. Cast off.

Several darts may be made at the same time. As an example, make four darts, two either side of the centre, as follows. Make transfers for the centre right dart as above, moving the stitches to the left. Make transfers for the outside right dart, moving the stitches to the left. Make transfers for the inside left dart, moving the stitches to the right. Make transfers for the outside left dart, moving the stitches to the right.

Curved shapes, e.g. yokes, may be knitted by making long darts spaced across the whole width of the knitting, although it is a much slower process than knitting sideways with horizontal darts. Figure 60 shows a detail of a patterned yoke pullover knitted by this method.

Similarly, increases may be made in the middle of the knitting by transferring stitches out. A stitch is picked up onto the empty needle as in fully fashioned increasing.

Contrast stitch shaping

Slight increases and decreases of width are possible by changing the stitch tension row by row. More pronounced shaping or even gathering is possible by a change both of tension and thickness of yarn, or by changing the stitch. A ribbed edge which is made tighter than the main knitting is the most common example of this, but ribbing may be introduced in the middle of a shape too, at the waist for instance. Other stitches have the effect of increasing the width in contrast to plain knitting, e.g. tuck or weaving.

Figure 60 Patterned yoke pullover

Creating Patterns

Tension swatch

Getting the size right is more difficult and more crucial in knitting than getting the shape perfect. It depends almost entirely on knitting and measuring a tension swatch correctly. Knit a 15cm (6 inch) square in the stitch, yarn and tension on which you have decided. If several different yarns or stripes of different stitches are to be used then they must be included in the swatch in the proportion in which they will be used to knit the garment. If a different fabric is to be used for front and back or body and sleeves, a separate swatch must be knitted for each.

Pull the swatch gently lengthways to even the spacing of the stitches. Finish the swatch in the same way as the garment is to be finished. This will normally mean blocking, but with oiled wool, for example, it will also mean washing. Detailed instructions are included in the chapter 'Finishing and Making Up'. Be careful not to stretch swatches when pinning them out for blocking, which is easy to do with such small pieces. The edges will stretch more than the centre, so they must be eased in, to match the proportions of the stitches in the middle. If this is not done correctly, a garment several sizes too small may result.

When the swatch is dry and relaxed after washing and/or blocking, measure the number of rows in 10cm (4 inches) and the number of stitches in 10cm (4 inches). Take the measurement from the centre of the swatch, as the stitches near the edge may be distorted and give a wrong count.

With tuck and slip stitch, the number of rows visible in the swatch will be less than the number of rows knitted. In all-over patterns, which are most common in these stitches, the solution is simple. Count the rows visible on the technical face side. Now calculate from the pattern what fraction of stitches are knitted in one wale. In a simple bird's eye pattern, for example, the fraction is a half. Turn the fraction upside down and multiply the rows

counted by this number. In this example the row count will be twice the number actually counted. With more complicated patterns it is easiest to measure the length of one repeat in the knitting, count up the total number of rows knitted for one repeat, and work out the proportion of rows counted to rows knitted from these two figures.

There is a similar problem with needle out knitting. To avoid confusion, patterns should always be worked out according to the number of needles over which the knitting is stretched. For example, in a swatch that was knitted with every third needle out, there are 20 stitches in 10cm (4 inches). Two thirds of all needles were knitting, so $3/2 \times 20 = 30$ needles in 10cm (4 inches). If this figure is always used, the numbering on the needle bed may still be used, and irregular needle out sequences will present no particular problem.

Drawing patterns

The following measurements are required for a pullover or cardigan: centre back length, bust, underarm length, width of shoulder from centre back, width at top of sleeve, armhole, width of sleeve at wrist, neckband over all, and width of neck at back from shoulder seam to shoulder seam. Ideally these measurements would be taken from an old garment that fits as required. If this is not possible, take the measurements direct from the figure to be fitted and adjust accordingly. The cuff should be wide enough to go over the fist, and the neck big enough to go over the head in pullovers. This is especially important in children's sizes. A neat fit at the neck and wrist depend on the elasticity of the band, not on a small initial measurement. No allowance for room need be made if a neat fit is wanted. However 2 to 5cm (1 to 2 inches) extra must be allowed in the length as knitwear tends to ride up.

If you have a knit tracer with ready-made patterns, they should be checked against these measurements and corrected if necessary. Plain paper may be used to draw patterns for knit tracers. Squared paper is best if a knit tracer is not to be used. It does not matter what size squares are used, but the sheets should be big enough to draw the shape full size.

Almost all pullovers and cardigans are made from simple rectangular shapes minus the armhole and neck shape. Different styles are created by changing the proportions rather than by changing the shape. To make a figure-hugging sweater, the width is based on a measurement slightly lesss than the actual bust size and the body is started with a narrow hem. Because of the elasticity of the knitting it will fit neatly all over. To make a big blouson-shaped jacket, take a measurement about 10cm (4 inches) greater than the bust, but start with a wide tight rib to gather the fullness onto the hip.

Other pattern shapes may be traced from dressmaking patterns or old garment pieces, and then simplified and adjusted to make them suitable for knitting, e.g. by making the front and back shapes identical. Some panels of a dressmaking pattern may be converted to a knitting pattern, e.g. front panels or sleeves of knitting in a leather or woven fabric jacket.

The following woman's measurements are used in the instructions in this chapter. Bust 85cm/34in. (82.5+2.5cm/33+1in. for room), length 60cm/24in. (55+5cm/22+2in. for room), underarm 40cm (16in.), shoulder 17.5cm (7in.), armhole 40–45cm (16–18in.) depending on the style of the sleeve, wrist 25cm (10in.), back of neck 17.5cm (7in.), neck over all 47.5cm (19in.). Length, bust and underarm length vary greatly from person to person, but the smaller measurements vary only slightly. Men's and children's measurements are quite different of course.

Body

The back and front will be identical except for neck shaping. Draw a rectangle 60cm × 42.5cm (24 × 17in.) (fig. 61). Draw a vertical centre line. Draw a line 5cm (2in.) up from the bottom line for the rib or hem (line a). If you are using squared paper, use a grid line for the centre line, but do not worry if the other lines do not coincide with the squares. This rectangle is the basis of all patterns.

Neck

The simplest neckline to make is a slit. Mark an opening 24cm (9½in.) wide (half neck). If the front

and back are finished at the top with a hem, there is no need to make a collar band or facing. The neck line can be brought forward for a better fit by making the back 2.5cm (1 inch) longer than the front (line b). If a crew neck is to be added, triangular gussets approximately 5cm (2in.) wide should be knitted and inserted on either side of the opening.

For a round neck, mark a point 9cm (3½in.) (half back of neck) either side of the centre and down from the top. Connect these points with a semi-circle (line c). Check that the over-all neck measurement is correct. If it is not, adjust the curve to increase or decrease it. In most cases the back may be knitted straight. For fine knitting it is better to draw a slight shaping for the back of the neck (line d).

For a 'V' neck mark a point on the centre line at the level of the bottom of the 'V'. This is best determined by measuring from the shoulder down on the figure to be fitted. Allow for the width of the band to be fitted. Mark 9cm (3½in.) either side of centre at the top. Draw a line between these three points (line e).

As well as making round and 'V' necks one of these two neck shapes will be suitable for all the various styles of collar. To convert any pattern to a coat or cardigan, knit the right and left front parts separately, and reduce the width at the centre by half the width of the button band, if one is to be added (line f).

If a button band is to be added to a pullover with or without a collar, allowance for it must be made when drawing the neck shape (line g).

Armholes

As with the neck, the simplest form of armhole is a slit, which gives a dropped shoulder. Mark an opening 22.5cm (9in.) down (half armhole over all). To make a less pronounced dropped shoulder, draw a line parallel to the edge 2.5cm (1in.) in, and 20cm (8in.) long, so that 20+2.5cm=22.5cm (8+1in.=9in.) half armhole. Connect the bottom of this line to the edge with a horizontal line (line k). This armhole may also be used with a sloping shoulder line.

A set in sleeve must have a sloping shoulder line. Draw it from the neck edge at approximately the angle shown (line h). Draw a vertical line 17.5cm (7in.) out from centre. Draw a horizontal line in from the edge 2.5cm (1in.) long and 19cm (7½in.) down from the top of the rectangle. Draw a diagonal line up from this point to connect with the vertical (line i). Check the over-all armhole measurement.

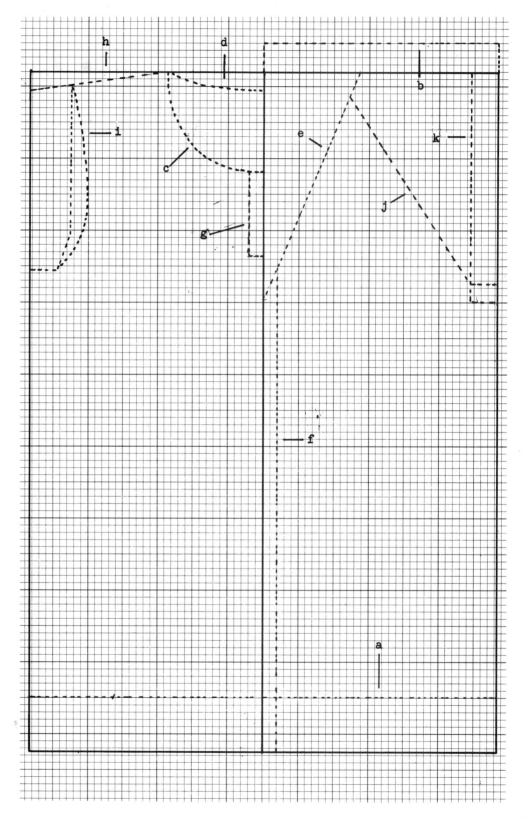

Figure 61
Body pattern

3   Short row technique used to make diagonal blocks of stripes

4　A tapestry in inlay technique

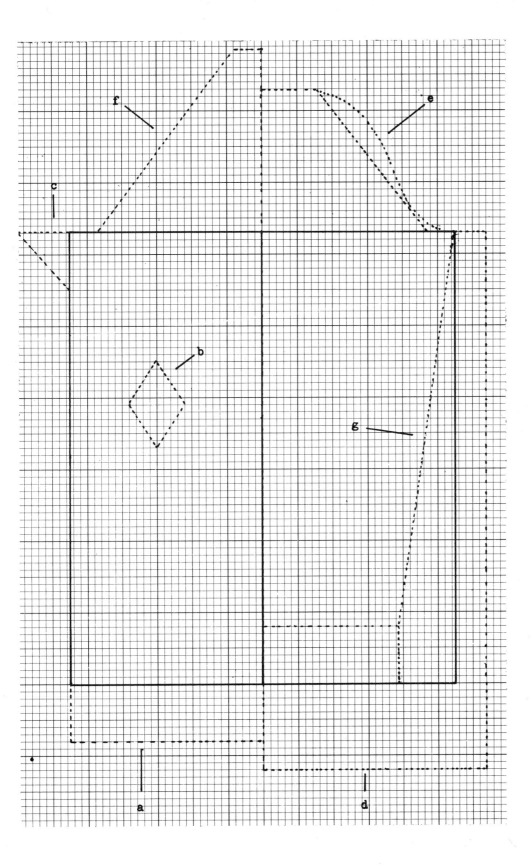

**Figure 62
Sleeve
pattern**

If the body is particularly narrow or the shoulder particularly wide, the armhole will be too small. Increase the over-all armhole measurement by drawing a curve between the same upper point down to the horizontal line.

To make a raglan shoulder, draw a horizontal line 19cm (7½in.) down from top to a point 2.5cm (1in.) in from the edge as in a set in sleeve hole. Join this point to a point 2.5cm (1in.) down on the neck line (line j).

Sleeves

The sleeve head must correspond to the type of armhole. As with body shapes, the simplest sleeve shape is a rectangle. All the following sleeve shapes are based on a rectangle 35 × 40cm (14 × 16in.) (fig. 62). For a sleeve to fit the dropped shoulder add 5cm (2in.) in length to the rectangle to make up for the lack of a sleeve head (line a). The length of the basic rectangle is based on the underarm measurement. Draw a separate diamond shape (b) 7.5 × 5cm (3 × 2in.). This is the gusset necessary to give underarm ease, and to make up the necessary width at the top. As an alternative to a gusset, extend the top of the sleeve either side by 5cm (2in.), and draw a line at 45 degrees into the sleeve (line c).

The semi-dropped shoulder has underarm ease by being set in. The rectangle must be 47.5cm (19in.) long (2.5cm/1in. added for the setting in) by 40cm (16in.) wide (line d).

For a set in sleeve, mark a point 2.5cm (1in.) in from the edge either side at the top. Extend the vertical centre line upwards by 12.5cm (5in.) (approximately three quarters of the height of the armhole). Draw a horizontal line and mark a point 5cm (2in.) out from the centre. Draw a diagonal between the two points (line e). Check the over-all sleeve head measurement. It should be slightly more than the armhole measurement. If it is not, it may be increased by drawing a curve, and decreased by lowering the sleeve head.

For a raglan sleeve, extend the centre line 16cm (6½in.) upwards (the height of a raglan armhole). Draw a horizontal line to a point 2.5cm (1in.) out from the centre. Mark a point 2.5cm (1in.) in from the edge on the top of the rectangle. Draw a diagonal between these two points (line f). Check that the over-all armhole measurement matches the sleeve head. If it does not, to reduce, lower the sleeve head, and to increase, raise the sleeve head.

All types of sleeve may be tapered or flared, or reduced to half or three quarter length, and a rib, hem or turned cuff can be added according to the design (line g).

These basic shapes may be elaborated on and altered with experience. For example, a dolman shape is made by drawing the body and sleeve of a dropped-shoulder pattern all in one. A yoke shape is made by drawing the top of the body and the top of the sleeves of a raglan pattern all in one. Exact lines of seams are not as important as they are in dressmaking, as long as the over-all proportions are correct. All-over stitch patterns or stripes need not be drawn on the pattern, but the position of isolated or spaced stripes, or areas of pattern, should be indicated.

Writing patterns

If you have a knit tracer, there is no need to write a pattern. Trace the pattern shape onto the plastic sheet provided, insert it into the tracer, set the stitch and row gauges according to the tension swatch and begin knitting. The tracer will show how many stitches there should be knitting at the end of each row, so you will know whether to increase or decrease. On the Knitmaster and Studio radar the pattern must be scaled down to half size and, for symmetrical shapes, the right side only drawn. The pattern may be drawn on ordinary paper which has been cut down to the right width. Draw a margin 1.25cm (½in.) from the left edge, and use this as the centre line.

If you do not have a tracer, the drawn pattern must be converted to instructions stating how many stitches to cast on, how many rows to knit, and when to increase or decrease.

To calculate how many stitches to cast on, measure the width of the shape at the bottom edge. Multiply the number of centimetres (inches) by the number of stitches per 10cm (4in.) in the tension swatch and divide the answer by 10(4). If the answer is a fraction, go to the next higher number. If it is an odd number, go to the next higher even number. There is no allowance for seams in knitting patterns, so the slight increase will not make it too wide. To calculate how many rows to knit for a straight-sided shape, e.g. a body shape from hem to underarm, measure the length of the shape and multiply the number of centimetres (inches) by the number of rows per 10cm (4in.) in the tension swatch and divide the answer by 10(4).

Take the line g (fig. 62) as an example of increasing in a straight line. Measure along a vertical line the distance in centimetres (inches) from the top of the cuff to the level of the underarm, which in this case is 35cm (14in.). Multiply this by the number of rows per 10cm (4in.), say 40, and divide the answer by 10(4). This gives us a total number of rows for

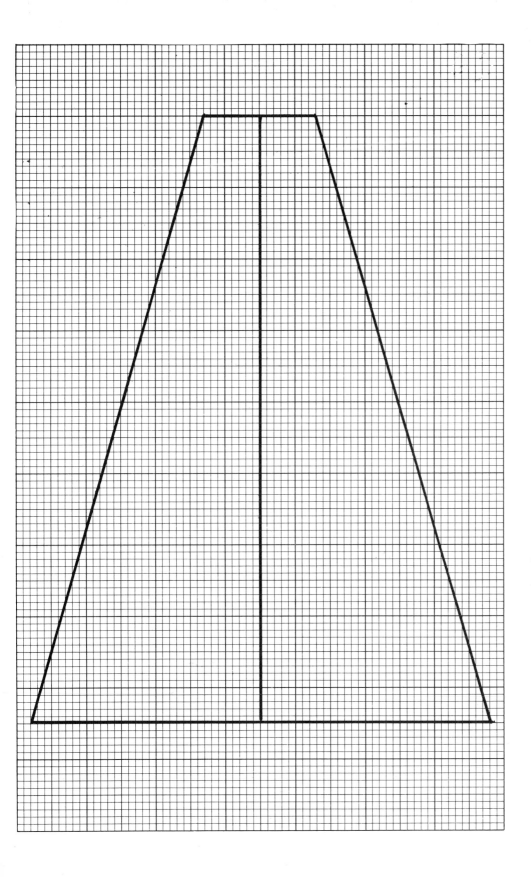

**Figure 63
Flared
skirt
pattern**

75

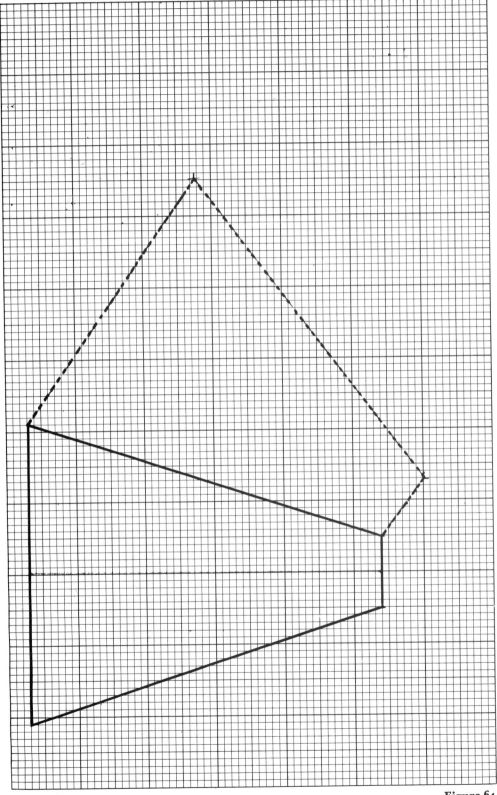

Figure 64

the underarm shaping of 140. Measure along a horizontal line the difference between the width of the sleeve at the cuff and at the underarm, which in this case is 5cm (2in.). Multiply this by the number of stitches per 10cm (4in.) in the tension swatch, say 24, and divide the answer by 10(4). This gives a total number of stitches to be increased of 12. Thus, 140 divided by 12 is 13 and 8 over. So you must knit 140 rows, increasing one stitch, both sides, every 13 rows.

Decreasing is worked out in the same way. Shallow angles are slightly different. Take line h in figure 61 as an example. Vertical distance is 1.25cm ($\frac{1}{2}$in.), which equals 5 rows. The amount to decrease is 9cm ($3\frac{1}{2}$in.) which equals 21 stitches. There are more stitches than rows, so several stitches must be decreased each row. More than one stitch at a time may only be decreased when the carriage is on that side, which will only happen twice in 5 rows. So the 21 stitches must be decreased in two goes, one of 11 stitches and one of 10.

Curved shaping is dealt with by dividing the curve into sections and treating each section separately as a straight line. A round neck as in line c (fig. 61) would be made up of a horizontal line, a shallow angle, a steeper angle and a vertical line.

Flared shapes

An example of a flared shape pattern is a flared skirt similar to the one shown in figure 59, to be knitted in six sections using the darting method (i.e. the sections will be knitted sideways in one continuous piece). The following measurements will be used: waist 60cm (24in.), hem 255cm (102in.), length 54cm (21$\frac{1}{2}$in.). The tension swatch has 24 stitches per 10cm (4in.) and 40 rows per 10cm (4in.).

Each section will measure 10cm (4in.) wide at the waist and 42.5cm (17in.) wide at the hem. Starting with a vertical centre line, draw this symmetrical shape (fig. 63). Turn the paper sideways and work out the knitting instructions (fig. 64), which are as follows. Cast on 2 stitches. Knit 65 rows increasing 4 stitches on the right every other row. Knit 40 rows. Knit 65 rows, decreasing 4 stitches every other row by the holding method. Knit 65 rows, increasing 4 stitches every other row by bringing the needles back to the knitting position. Complete six sections in this way, and use the casting off method of decreasing for the last section. For a perfect finish, start and end on waste yarn, using the holding method for all increasing and decreasing, and graft the seam:

Details and Trims

Bottom edges

A simple cast on edge will curl and stretch however carefully it is steamed. A sewn hem will prevent this, but a knitted hem is neater and quicker. Open cast on with waste yarn. Knit several rows. Set the tension to the selected number, say 7. Thread the main yarn. Knit one row. Change the tension to two numbers tighter, that is, 5. Knit 9 rows. Set the tension to 7. Knit one row. Set the tension to 5. Knit 10 rows. Pick up the first row of main yarn stitches onto the needles (figs. 65 and 66). Knit several rows, then unravel the waste yarn. Continue knitting. The hem is knitted at a tighter tension to keep it flat and firm. The first row is loose so that, when it is knitted in, it does not show through on the right side. The loose row in the middle makes a neat straight fold.

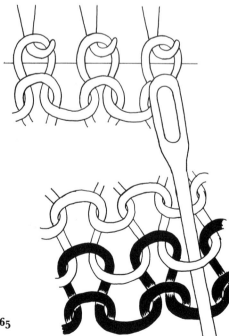

Figure 65

A picot hem is made by transferring every other stitch after knitting the middle row of the hem. When folded in half, this row of lace holes makes the picot effect.

Here is an example of how to knit a scalloped hem by the short row method. Open cast on 30 stitches with waste yarn. Knit several rows. Thread the main yarn. Knit two rows. Place the carriage on the right. Bring 20 left-hand needles to the forward hold position. Set the holding cam control on hold. Knit one row. Bring the first right-hand needle to the forward position. Knit one row. Bring the next needle at the left to the forward position. Continue knitting and bringing one needle to the holding position each row, until only one needle is knitting. Continue knitting, returning one needle to the knitting position each row until all 10 needles are knitting again. Finish with the carriage on the right. Bring the centre 10 needles to the knitting position. Knit one row. Bring 10 needles on the right to hold. Repeat the sequence of knitting point on the centre needles, and then on the 10 left-hand needles. Then bring all the needles to the knitting position. Knit two rows. Pick up the hem. Continue knitting.

Rib is made on a single bed machine by means of the latch hook. Cast on by hand. Drop every other cast on loop by moving the needle back to the non-knitting position. Knit 5 rows. Insert the latch hook upside down, above the bottom bar, beneath a non-knitting needle. Turn the hook the right way up, so that the yarn is twisted once round it. With the latch hook, knit this newly cast on stitch into the bar above (fig. 67). Continue upwards until all five bars have been knitted. Transfer the top stitch onto an empty needle. Knit up onto all empty needles in the same way. Continue knitting. Any type of rib may be knitted according to which cast on stitches are dropped.

To make a false 1 × 1 rib, follow the instructions for making a hem, but with the following differences.

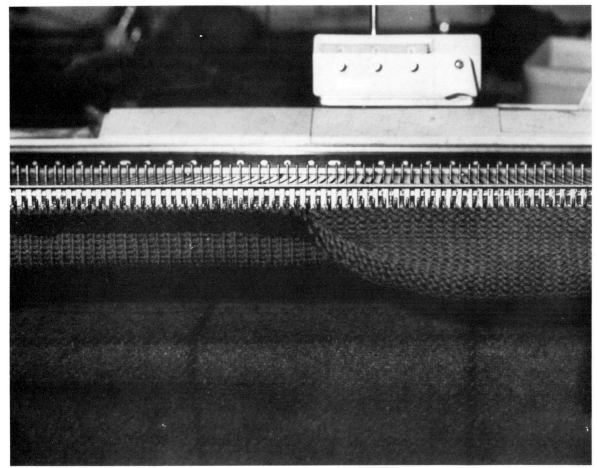

Figure 66 Picking up a hem

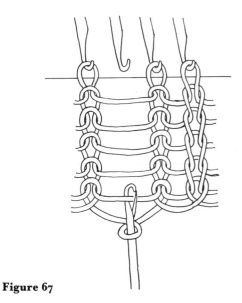

Figure 67

Cast on alternate needles only. When ready to pick up stitches, bring the remaining empty needles to the knitting position. Pick up the stitches onto the empty needles. Other types of rib may be made by the same method. For example, for a 2 × 1 rib, leave every third needle out when casting on. When picking up stitches, starting at the left, leave the first needle, and transfer the first stitch onto the second needle, and the second stitch onto the empty needle (fig. 68). Continue picking up stitches passing over

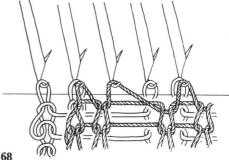

Figure 68

every third needle. A false rib is quicker to do than a true rib, but it is not so elastic and does not look so neat.

Neck bands

Neck bands may be made in three ways, corresponding to the three types of bottom edge, i.e. a tightly knitted band of plain knitting, latch tool rib, and false rib. Follow the instructions given for bottom edges, except to change to a loose tension on the last row and finish with waste yarn before removing from the needles. In the case of double bands, do not pick up the first row onto the needles, as the doubling will be done at the making up stage. Stretch the tension swatches for the neck bands widthways when counting the stitches, to ensure a neat fit.

Bands for round necks are simple rectangles which stretch to fit and have a join at one shoulder seam. Bands for 'V' necks may be shaped at either end to join at the centre front. For double bands, cast on the number of stitches required to fit the neck edge. Decrease one stitch fully fashioned each row at either side until the middle loose row. Then increase one stitch either side each row to the end. For a single rib band, cast on the number of stitches needed to fit the neck edge less the number of stitches to be increased. For a band 10 rows wide, this would be less 10 stitches either side. Knit 10 rows increasing one stitch either side each row.

Bands for squared necks are made in a similar way, but the band must be made in several pieces. For example, a neck line which was squared at the front and the back would require four pieces, one for either side and one each for front and back. It is only necessary to increase and decrease one stitch every other row when shaping the corners of a square neck band.

An easy method for making bands for 'V' and square necks is to knit straight pieces and overlap the join, stitching either end into the opposite side of the 'V'.

Front edges

The simplest way of finishing the front edge of a cardigan is to add about 5cm (2 inches) to the width at the centre front and turn a hem. This is quite adequate for a zipper jacket, as the zip tape will prevent the edge from stretching. A neater finish would be to add a more tightly knitted facing, with the zip set between the facing and the turned edge. The methods described for bottom edges may

all be used for front edges. Double edges in plain tight knitting may also be made longways instead of widthways, but they are more difficult to join neatly.

Knitted cord may be used as an edging either round or pressed flat. Cast on four stitches. Place the carriage at the right. Set all the needles to slip when knitting right to left, and set all the needles to knit when knitting left to right. Set the tension fairly tight. As the knitting progresses the floats across the front will close to form circular knitting.

Buttonholes

A single lace stitch makes a small buttonhole. To make a buttonhole two stitches wide, transfer the left stitch one needle to the left, and the right stitch one needle to the right. Knit one row. Drop the loose yarn from both needles. Wind it round each empty needle as in casting on (fig. 69). Knit one row. Make sure the two newly cast on stitches have knitted down. If not, knit them down by hand. Continue knitting.

Here are examples of buttonholes made over three needles. They may be made to any width required.

(a) Lay a length of spare yarn in the hook of one needle. Knit this stitch into the spare yarn. Using the end of the spare yarn, cast off three stitches to the left by the transfer tool method, and then cast on again on the empty needles (fig. 70). Knit one row. Make sure the newly cast on stitches have knitted down. If they have not, knit them down by hand. Continue knitting.

(b) Pick up a stitch with the latch hook, and, using the latch hook method, cast off three stitches to the left. Knit one row. Use the yarn float across the empty needles to cast on new stitches, as in the two-stitch buttonhole (fig. 71). Knit one row. Make sure the new stitches have knitted down. If not, knit them down by hand.

(c) Take a length of yarn in a contrasting colour and knit it into the three stitches by hand (fig. 72). Continue knitting. Finish knitting and remove from the machine. Steam the buttonhole and pull out the waste yarn. Hold the stitches by the straight thread cast off method. Tie off the cast off thread so as to give a hole exactly the right size for the button. Finish in buttonhole stitch.

Vertical buttonholes are made by the short row method. To make a buttonhole four rows long, with the carriage on the right, bring all the needles to the left of the buttonhole position to the forward hold position. Set the holding cam control to hold. Knit

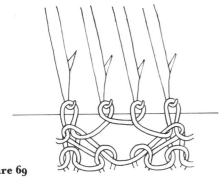

Figure 69

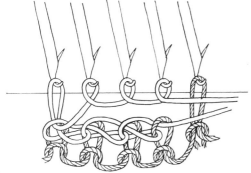

Figure 70

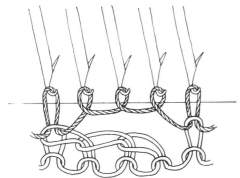

Figure 71

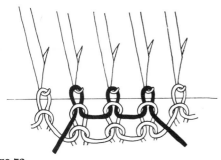

Figure 72

four rows. Break the yarn. Bring the right-hand needles to the forward hold position. Pass the empty carriage to the left-hand side. Bring all the needles left of the buttonhole position back to the knitting position. Re-thread the yarn. Knit four rows. Set the holding cam control to knit in. Continue knitting.

The need to make buttonholes can be avoided by leaving gaps when joining a front band to a front edge, by making loops with knitted cord, or by making a loop of yarn finished in buttonhole stitch. A buttonhole attachment may be used on a sewing machine to make buttonholes in knitting; it is quick and gives a neat finish.

Collars

A crew or polo neck is simply an extended neckband. It must be in real or double rib to be elastic enough to go over the head and still fit neatly at the neck.

The pattern for a cutaway collar is a simple rectangle (fig. 73). It must be in rib as the curved collar shape is achieved by stretching the outer edge. For the same reason it must be knitted widthways and not lengthways. Cast on at line a for a single collar in true rib and finish with waste yarn. Start and finish with waste yarn for a double rib and start at line b. In some yarns a double rib will be too bulky for a collar. In this case knit a single collar in false rib and stitch a small hem one or two rows wide to finish the edge. Sides of double collars are normally closed by seaming. Pull the collar tension swatch lengthways to close the rib when counting stitches. Calculate the number of stitches required to cast on by multiplying the number of stitches per 10cm (4in.) in the tension swatch by the length of the neck edge and divide the answer by 10(4). With a false rib or any rib with little stretch, add 2.5cm (1 inch) and ease into the neck edge when making up.

To make a pointed collar, add about 5cm (2 inches) to the outer edge measurement and decrease into the neck edge c (fig. 73). Be sure in latch hook rib to knit up purl stitches at the edge before decreasing over them. This simple shape makes the points rather long in relation to the width of the collar. The points may be reduced by shaping the outside edge d. To make a neat edge cast on the number of stitches required for the total width of collar. Knit two rows, and then shape by the holding method. With the carriage at the right, bring the left-hand needles up to point e to hold. Knit one row. Bring the same number of needles to hold on the right. Continue knitting, increasing

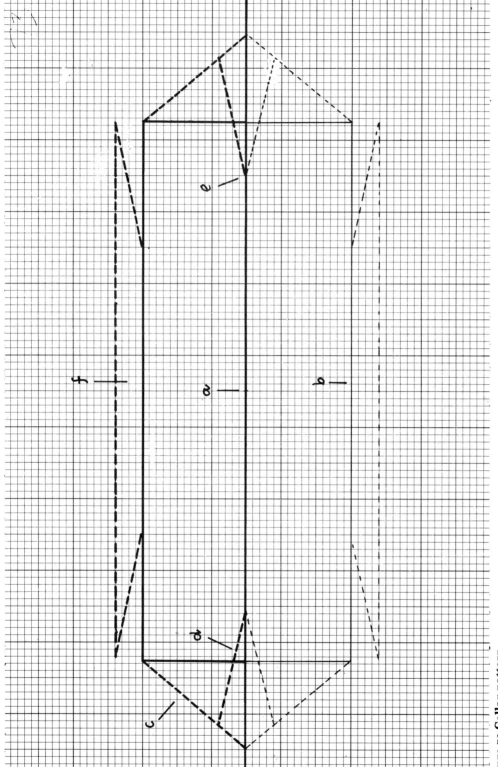

Figure 73 Collar pattern

according to the pattern by returning the needles to the knitting position. Decrease into the neck by the normal method. To make a double collar to this pattern, cast on and increase to the point in the normal way. Do the shaping at the fold line by the holding method. Decrease into the neck in the normal way.

An alternative to shaping the outer edge is to make the whole collar narrower and to add a wedge-shaped neck band to give the necessary height at the back (f). It may either be knitted separately or all in one by the holding method.

All these collars may be used with 'V' or square necks as well as with round necks. Shawl or roll collars, and collars with revers fit onto 'V' necks. The simplest pattern for either a full length roll collar on a cardigan or a set in collar in a pullover, is a rectangle knitted sideways in rib (fig. 74). This gives a wide overlap in front (fig. 75). Because the maximum width of the machine is about 75cm (30 inches), a full length collar must be knitted in two parts with a join at the centre back. Add together half the back of the neck, the length of the 'V', and the front edge measurements to calculate the width. Allow enough, when calculating the number of rows to knit, to give a generous roll.

For a roll collar with a narrow front band the collar width a is tapered from halfway down the 'V' (fig. 74). The holding method of shaping already described for pointed collars may be used for double rib. Roll collars set into pullovers will fit 'V' or square necks or a cut off 'V' shape which is a cross between the two.

If a roll collar is to be knitted lengthways, some shaping is required at the top of the 'V', as the outside edge of a collar knitted this way will not stretch enough to allow it to curve round the neck. Knit up to the top of the 'V' straight, then turn the collar by knitting a wedge by the short row method. Continue knitting straight to the centre back, or if the collar is being knitted in one piece, up to the top of the 'V' on the opposite side. Repeat the shaping and continue straight to the end (fig. 76).

Revers or lapels are made all in one with the button band, but may be made separate from or all in one with the collar. To make a pattern for separate revers, start by drawing the 'V' and front edge of the cardigan to be fitted. Draw a button band of the required width up to the bottom of the 'V'. Draw a horizontal line out from the 'V' about 5cm (2 inches) down from the top.

Mark the width of revers required along this line. Draw a line from this point to the top of the button band (fig. 77). Knit sideways. For a single thickness

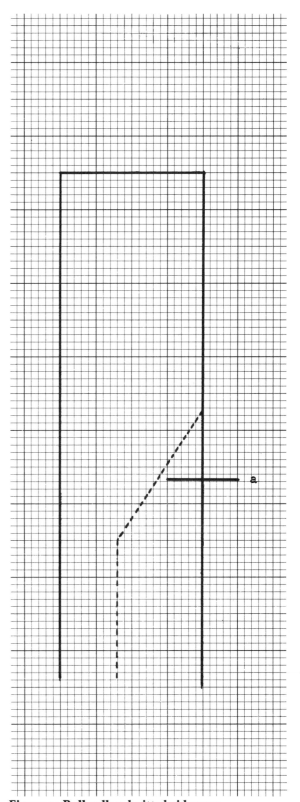

Figure 74 Roll collar, knitted sideways

83

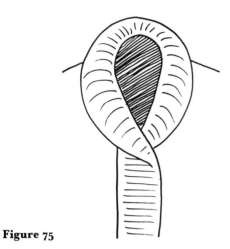

Figure 75

rib start at the outside edge and finish on waste yarn. For double thickness revers start at the inside edge. Shape the outside by the holding method and finish on the inside again. The collar, which may be square or pointed, is made in the normal way and is set on the neck edge and along the top of the revers at either side (fig. 78).

Collar and revers made all in one would be knitted lengthways. To make the pattern, start by drawing the front edge and 'V' of the cardigan to be fitted. Draw a button band of required width up to the bottom of the 'V'. Draw the revers as in figure 77. Extend the top of the 'V' by half the measurement of the back of the neck. Draw a line out at right angles to this point and mark the width of collar required. Connect this point with the point of the revers. Draw a notch. Because this collar is knitted lengthways, it must be turned by the short row method at the top of the 'V' (fig. 79).

Figure 78

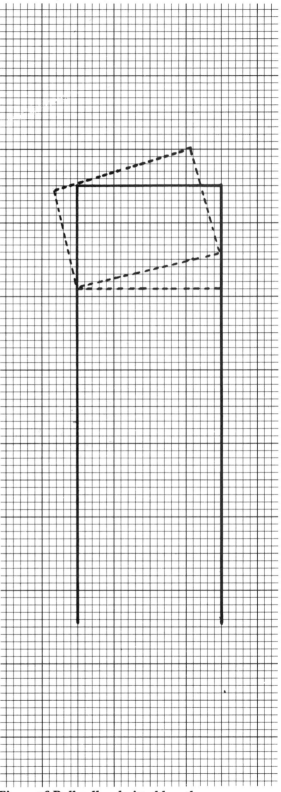

Figure 76 Roll collar, knitted lengthways

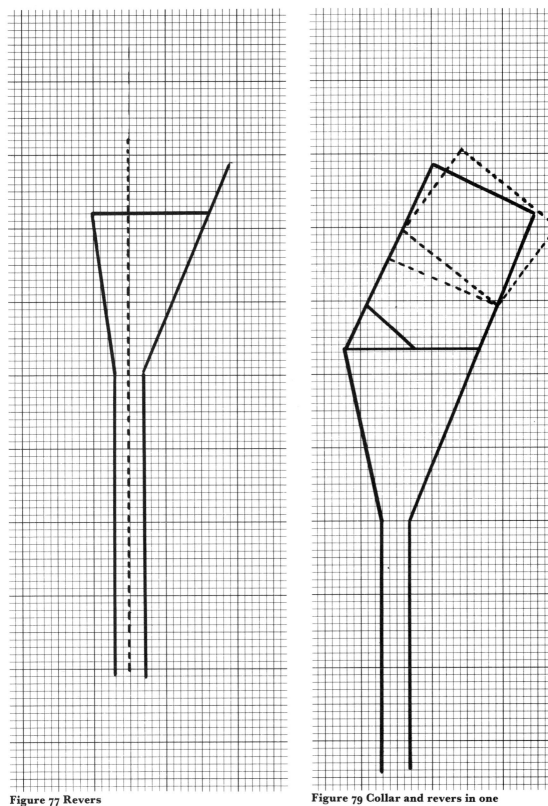

Figure 77 Revers

Figure 79 Collar and revers in one

Pockets

To make a knitted pocket follow the instructions on page 64 for a fold. Pull the fold through to the wrong side, stitch up the sides, and steam it flat. The top may be finished by any of the edging methods already described.

Patch pockets are knitted upside down, starting with a hem or rib, and attached by normal seaming stitch. For a diagonal or vertical opening patch pocket, the edging must be knitted separately.

For a set in pocket with a vertical or diagonal opening, a double pocket must be knitted separately. Follow the instructions for a vertical buttonhole to make a vertical pocket opening. Here is an example of how to make a diagonal opening. Cast on 30 stitches. Knit several rows. Finish with the carriage on the right. Bring 10 left-hand needles to the forward position. Set the holding cam control to hold. Knit 10 rows, decreasing one stitch at the left every other row by the casting off method. Break the yarn. Bring the remaining 10 right-hand needles to hold. Pass the carriage to the left of all the needles. Bring 10 left-hand needles to the knitting position. Knit 10 rows, increasing one stitch every other row at the right by the casting on method. When increasing, bring the needle only to position 'B', and wind the yarn round the in hook. Set the holding cam control to knit in. Continue knitting.

A knitted in flap for a patch pocket is made in the same way as a knitted pocket, except to pull the fold to the right side before stitching up the sides and steaming. Knit the flap at a tighter tension than the main knitting. A fold may be made long enough to make both the flap and pocket in one (fig. 80).

Here is another way to make a knitted in pocket with a flap. Cast on 30 stitches and knit several rows.

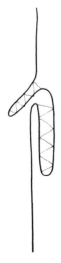

Figure 80

Finish with the carriage on the right. Bring 10 left-hand needles to the forward position. Set the holding cam control on hold. Knit one row. Bring 10 right-hand needles to the forward position. Break the yarn and re-thread the feeder with waste yarn. Knit several rows. Break the waste yarn and drop 10 centre stitches. Re-thread the main yarn and cast on 10 centre stitches with it. Make a flap of the required length by following the instructions for knitting a hem. Finish with the carriage on right. Bring all the left-hand needles to the knitting position. Knit one row. Set the holding cam control to knit in. Continue knitting to the end. Remove the knitting from the machine. Pick up the open stitches at the pocket opening onto the needles. Unravel the waste yarn. Knit a length for the pocket bag. Cast off. Fold, and sew the sides. Join the top edge to the top of the pocket opening.

Belts

Belts may be knitted lengthways or widthways. Knit twice the width required, fold and seam. Belts knitted lengthways tend to stretch and become longer and thinner in use. Widthways knitted belts may be knitted as if making a hem, starting with waste yarn. On the last row, pick the bottom row of open stitches, unravel the waste yarn, and cast off the beginning and end together. Ends generally look better if shaped to a point or wedge. A tie belt with fringed ends may be knitted widthways by pulling a long loop of yarn down beneath the carriage at the beginning of each row. Finish the fringe by cutting the loops off and tying the ends in bunches, or over stitch the end of the belt. Use a laying in yarn to get a fuller fringe.

Cord knitting will make a belt suitable for a light-weight garment. To make a bigger round belt cast on 15 or so stitches and allow the knitting to curl up naturally without steaming.

A rope belt to match is made as follows. Cut several lengths of yarn three times as long as the belt required. Tie them together at one end and hook the knot on a door handle or hook in the wall. Take opposite ends, pull tight, and twist in the opposite direction to the twist of the yarn, until the yarn begins to kink. The twisting is best done by tying the ends of yarn to a stick or long pencil, holding the yarn bunched in the left fist, and the winding stick (like a propeller) with the right hand. Keeping the yarns taught, fold in half so that the two ends twist firmly together. Trim irregular ends, and knot together.

There are several ways to attach belts to garments.

Knit a row of lace holes and thread a cord or rope belt into them. Knit a facing slightly wider than the belt to make a tunnel for the belt. Bring the belt ends to the front of the garment through a vertical buttonhole in the appropriate place. Belt loops could be made of cord or yarn worked in buttonhole stitch.

Fringes

Here is an example of how to knit fringing, which may be used as a trimming for scarves, shawls etc. Bring 40 needles to the knitting position. Push back out of the knitting the 30 centre needles, leaving 5 needles in the knitting position on either side. Cast on and knit several rows. Cut through the middle of the long floats and remove from the machine, so making two lengths of fringing. Weaving is particularly suitable for fringing because the ends are then closely spaced, and are also less likely to unravel.

Hand knitted trim

There is no reason why machine knitting should not be finished off by hand, either with knitting or crochet. Hand knitted ribs may be transferred to the needle bed, open stitches may be picked up off the machine onto needles, or loops picked up at the sides to add knitted or crocheted details.

Finishing and Making Up

Blocking

Before sewing knitted pieces together they are normally blocked, i.e. pinned out to shape and steamed. Blocking serves two purposes. One is to flatten curly fabric. The other is to fix the shape of the stitches to make a more stable fabric. It is very time consuming, and is not always necessary or even advisable. Bulky fabrics, or fabrics which are naturally stable such as tightly knit weave or tuck, do not benefit. Fine plain knitting generally requires blocking to give it shape and fit. True rib which is required to be elastic (e.g. neckbands) should not be blocked. True rib which is required to keep a fixed dimension (e.g. button bands) should be blocked.

A surface is required which is soft enough so that the natural texture and softness of the fabric is not impaired, but which is firm enough to hold pins. It must also be big enough for the largest knitted shape to be laid out. It is possible to use several layers of blanket, but they must be stretched out and held in some way. If they are laid loosely on a table they will move, and pins will pull loose, causing the knitting to lose its shape. The best and simplest solution is to use a piece of carpet, especially the modern bonded type, or a sheet of fairly hard foam, with a cloth laid on top.

Pin the piece of knitting out exactly to the pattern shape, face down. Check all the measurements and that it is all square, or, if you have one, lay a full size pattern on the steam table and pin the knitting on top of it. Pin the whole shape first with a few pins making sure the main measurements are correct, and then put a pin every 2.5cm (1 inch) all round to give an exact outline (fig. 81).

Pin into the very edge stitch, and with the pin angled outwards. There may be loose folds of fabric in the middle if it has stretched during knitting. Do not worry about this. They will disappear during steaming. Lay a really wet cotton cloth over the knitting. Hold an iron, set at full heat, above the cloth so that it just touches, but without its weight being felt by the cloth. The steam produced will do the job. Pressure is not necessary, and will have a detrimental effect on the texture and handle of the knitting. Lift the iron and put it down again until the whole area has been covered.

Do not slide the iron in contact with the cloth, or the fabric may be distorted. If there is still loose fabric in the centre after steaming, flatten it and ease it away with the hand. Similarly if the knitting was small and had to be stretched to shape, ease it outwards with the hands. In either case wet the cloth and steam a second time. Leave pinned out until absolutely dry. This will take quite a long time with certain fibres, particularly wool.

Never put pins along an edge which is going to show in the made up garment (e.g. the bottom of a hem) as it will leave an uneven edge. Pin along the top edge of the hem, but still steam the unpinned hem. As ribs should not be blocked, pin along the top edge and only steam down to the pins.

If oiled wool has been used, wash the pieces before making up, lay them flat on a towel to dry, and then block them while they are still slightly damp. Fabrics of waxed yarn should not need washing out. All fibres except acrylic may be blocked in the same way. Although a hot iron would have a detrimental effect on some fibres the temperature of the steam which penetrates the cloth does not. This is another reason for being quite certain not to press onto the cloth with the iron. Acrylic is affected by steam and must be therefore be lightly pressed with a dry cloth, and with the iron on a moderate heat.

Double ribs may be lightly steamed without pinning as for hems, but for maximum elasticity they need special treatment. Gather the fabric about 5cm (2 inches) above the top of the rib and pin to the steam table. Insert a metal ruler or other flat strip of metal between the two layers of rib, and use it to pull the rib longer. At the same time gather the rib

Figure 81 Pinning out for blocking

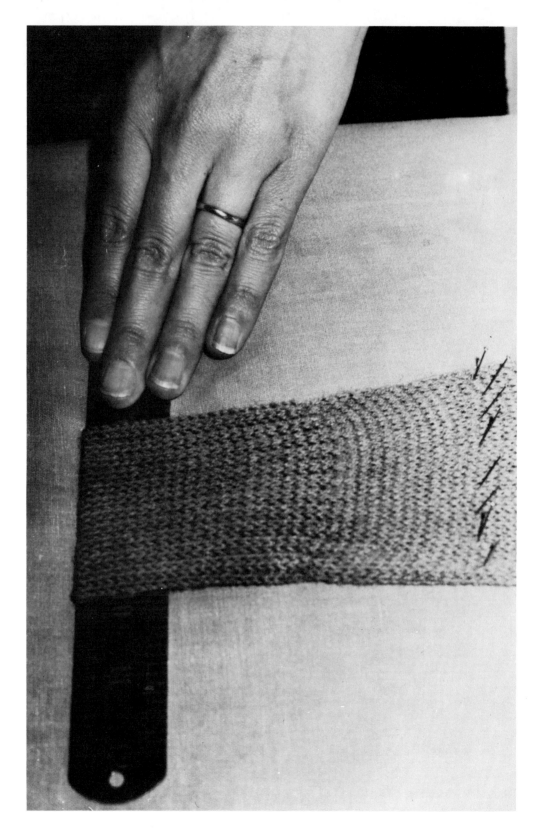

Figure 82
Pulling out
the rib

together at the bottom edge (fig. 82). Keep the rib pulled out, and place a wet cloth over it. Place the iron over the cloth for barely a second. Remove the cloth, and leave the rib to dry.

All trims finished with waste yarn, whether they are blocked or not, must have their open edges lightly steamed before removing the waste yarn, to prevent the open edge unravelling during sewing. Collars should not be blocked before making up, as they would less easily take up their curved shape.

Sewing

Knitwear is most easily made up in the following order: make one shoulder seam (for cardigans, both shoulder seams); attach the right side of the neck band or collar and turn; make the second shoulder seam, including the closing neck band; set in the sleeves; make the arm and side seam all in one; attach the right side of the front bands (if any) and turn.

A blunt knitwear needle threaded with the knitting yarn is used to sew into the stitches without splitting the yarn. If the knitting yarn is highly textured, a matching plain yarn may be used. Fine yarns or weak yarns such as shetland should be used double. Pin the edges to be sewn together first, as it is easy to stretch one side more than the other. This is particularly important where one edge is being eased into another, e.g. the sleeve head into the arm hole, or the neck edge into the ribbed neck band. Stitches must not be pulled too tight. There should be as much stretch in the seam as in the body of the knitting. If there is not, undue strain will be put on the join, and the garment will not hang properly.

Stitches

Mattress stitch

Mattress stitch or invisible seaming is the most useful seaming stitch. It is possible to make an absolutely invisible join of two vertical edges (e.g. a side seam). It is not bulky, and may be made loose enough to stretch with the knitting without gaping when relaxed. As it is worked from the right side, stripes and patterns may be matched exactly and hems joined neatly inside and out.

Hold the two pieces to be joined edge to edge, with the right side towards you. Work from right to left. Pass the needle under two bars, one stitch in from the edge of the top piece, and then under the corresponding bars, one stitch in from the edge of the lower piece. Then pass it back into the same hole in

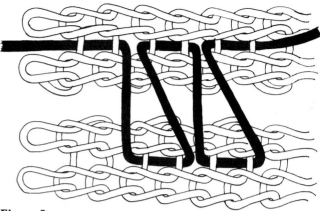

Figure 83

the top piece and under two bars (fig. 83).

Continue for several stitches quite loosely. Then pull the thread to bring the edges together, and immediately stretch the seam out again. The seam will then be as elastic as the knitting. Follow the same procedure for shaped edges, putting the needle in parallel to the edge approximately one stitch in. With hems or double ribs, start on the wrong side at the top of the hem, work down to the bottom edge and up the outside.

Crochet chain stitch

Crochet chain stitch with a latch hook or a crochet hook is a quick method of seaming, although not as neat as mattress. Hold the two edges with the right sides together. Work from right to left. Insert the hook and latch through both thicknesses one or two stitches in from the edge. Place the end of the yarn in the hook and pull a loop through the fabric. Push the hook through the fabric again two stitches along. Pull a new loop through the fabric and the first stitch (fig. 84). Continue. At the end of the seam break the yarn and pull the end through the last stitch to tie off.

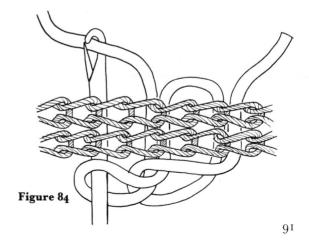

Figure 84

Back stitch

Back stitch is used to sew open edges onto closed edges (e.g. neckband to neck edge). A double band is joined on the right side first with back stitch, and then turned and hemmed on the inside. It is used to cast off rib, and may be used for non-stretch seams, e.g. to prevent shoulder seams drooping. When sewing open edges, all the stitches must be picked up or they will run. Steam the waste knitting and the first row or two of the band.

Unpick the waste knitting except for the last row. With both body and band face up, pin the band on top of the neck edge overlapping by approximately two rows. Starting at the right, unravel two or three stitches of waste yarn. Thread the needle with the knitting yarn doubled. Pass the needle down into the first open stitch of the band and through the neck edge behind, then up through the neck edge and the second open stitch. Take the needle down into the first stitch and the neck edge again, and up through the third stitch, then down through the second stitch, and up through the fourth stitch. Continue, unravelling the waste yarn a few stitches ahead all the time (fig. 85).

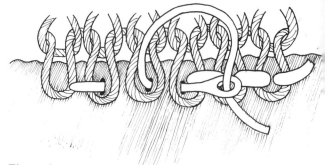

Figure 85

Hemming stitch

Hemming stitch is used for sewn hems, to turn down top edges, and for turning double bands. When turning open edges be sure to sew into every stitch. Steam the edge, and unravel all but the last row of waste. Turn and pin the hem. Starting at the right, unravel two or three stitches of waste yarn. Pass the needle down into the first open stitch and under the loop of corresponding stitch of the main knitting (fig. 86). Do not pull tightly. The hem should be invisible from the right side. Continue, unravelling the waste yarn a few stitches ahead all the time.

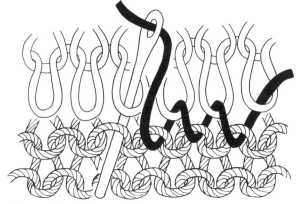

Figure 86

Grafting

Grafting is used to join two open edges, e.g. shoulders finished on waste yarn, or an open edge to a closed edge. If neatly done it is quite invisible, as it imitates a row of knitting. Hold the two pieces of knitting edge to edge, face up. Starting at the right, pass the needle down through the first stitch and up through the second stitch in the top edge, down through the first stitch and up through the second stitch in the bottom edge, then down through the second stitch and up through the third stitch in the top edge, and so on (fig. 87).

Buttonhole stitch

Buttonhole stitch is used to finish off open stitch buttonholes, and to make belt or button loops. To

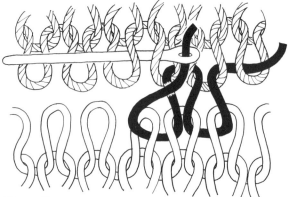

Figure 87

make a loop, start with a bridge of thread the required size. Stitch back and forth several times. Then, to make buttonhole stitch, starting on the left, pass the needle up behind the bridge threads, and forward through the loop of sewing thread. Continue, making stitches close together (fig. 88). To finish off a buttonhole, start by bringing the needle up through the edge of the hole, and then forward through the loop of sewing thread.

Figure 88

Blanket stitch

Blanket stitch is made in a similar way to buttonhole stitch, but with the stitches spaced out. It is used to secure cut edges and, with several thicknesses of yarn in a contrasting colour, to make a decorative feature of a seam, or as a decorative edging. It is only suitable for heavier fabrics. Hold the pieces edge to edge, face up. Starting at the left, pass the needle down through the lower piece about 1–2cm ($\frac{1}{4}$–$\frac{1}{2}$ inch) in from the edge, and up through the upper fabric, as close to the edge as possible. Bring the needle forward through the loop of sewing thread (fig. 89).

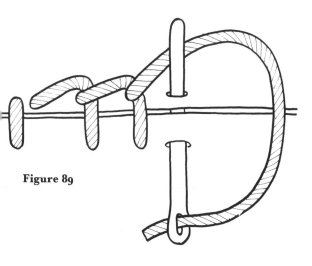

Figure 89

Machine zigzag stitch

Seams may be machine sewn. Synthetic yarn is best because it has more stretch than cotton. Machined seams are unattractive and impractical for heavy or bulky knitting as they compress the fabric and do not allow enough elasticity. Zigzag stitch allows more give in the seam, and is more suitable than straight stitching. Use a small zigzag for fine fabrics, and a larger zigzag for heavier fabrics. Ease the fabric under the sewing foot gently, and never pull it through, as over stretching and buckling will result.

Steaming seams

After making up, gently steam the outside of seams and the inside of hems and turns. Steam shoulder seams in the round, either on a dress stand, the end of a sleeve board or ironing board, or even on the wearer. Puckers on the shoulder or other seams can be steamed and eased away with the hand. Collars or other rounded parts should also be steamed and stretched into shape in the round.

Constructing on the machine

There are various ways of reducing the amount of making up necessary. Several pattern shapes may be knitted all in one. Knit the back and fronts of a cardigan sideways all in one starting at the centre of the right front, and finishing at the centre of the left front (fig. 90). Waist shaping is possible by the darting method. Sew a hem or add a rib.

Knit the front and back of a pullover all in one by starting at the bottom front and finishing at the bottom back (fig. 91). Slope the shoulders, if necessary, by darting. Knit the body and sleeve in one, sideways if a long sleeve is required (fig. 92). Knit the collar and button band as one shape.

One shape may be knitted directly onto another. To knit a button band onto a front edge, calculate the number of stitches required and bring them to the knitting position in the normal way. Hold the left front edge of the cardigan up against the needle bed with the face side towards the machine. Insert the transfer tool into the edge under the first stitch at the left (at the neck end), and transfer onto the first left-hand needle. Repeat at the right-hand side. Pick up a stitch in the middle of the edge and transfer onto the centre needle (fig. 93). Pick up and transfer to the machine loops in the middle of the right and left halves. The knitting is now evenly spaced across the needle bed. Pick up loops onto the remaining needles. Knit the band in the normal way, and finish on waste yarn. Turn and hem stitch.

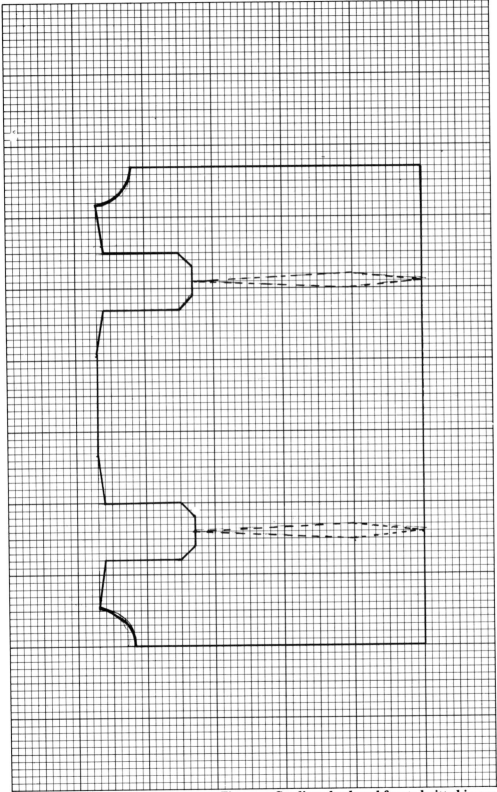

Figure 90 Cardigan back and fronts knitted in one

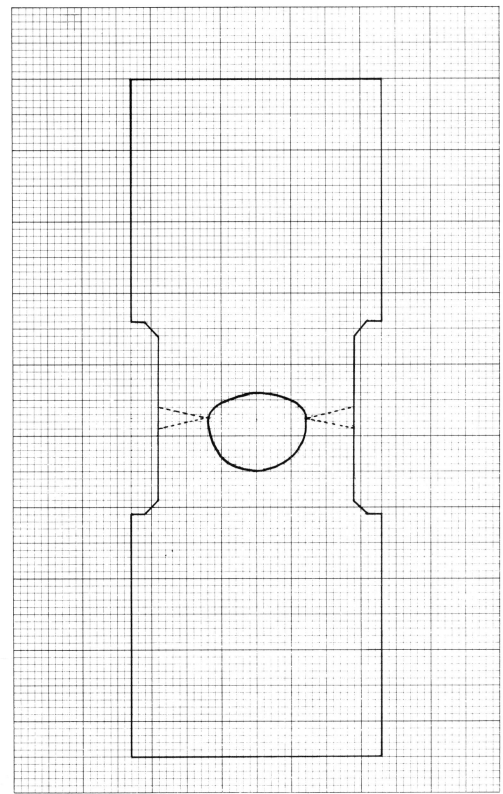

Figure 91 Pullover front and back knitted in one

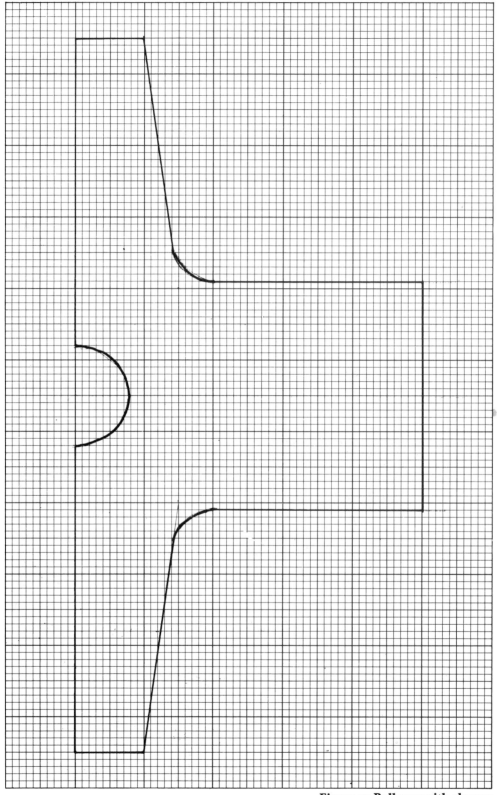

Figure 92 Pullover with sleeves

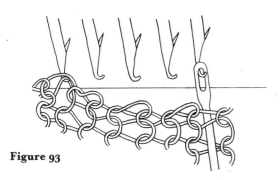

Figure 93

As an alternative, the front edge may be hung on the needles with the right side away from the machine. The band must then be turned outwards and back stitched. This is a slower method, but gives a better finish if done neatly.

Neck edges may be picked up to knit neckbands and collars in the same way. Sew one shoulder seam on a round-necked pullover before picking up onto the needles. Knit the band. Sew the second shoulder seam and join the band at the same time. Turn and stitch down the band. Sew both shoulder seams on a 'V' neck. Pick up the left side of the neck edge from the centre front to the centre back, and knit the left half of the band. Repeat for the right half. Join the band at the centre front and the centre back. Turn and stitch down.

Other joins may be made in the same way, e.g. on a dropped sleeve, sew the shoulder seam, pick up the armhole onto the needles, and knit the sleeve downwards. Pieces may be joined side by side on the machine too, e.g. knit the front pieces of a cardigan. Cast on stitches for the back. Knit one row. Pick the edge stitch in the first row of the left front onto the first needle on the right. Pick the edge stitch in the first row of the right front onto the first needle on the left. Continue knitting back, picking up the edge stitches from the fronts onto the needles until the armhole is reached.

Patch pockets may be knitted directly onto the body in the following way. Knit the front. On the row level with the bottom of the intended pocket, feed a contrasting coloured yarn in with the main knitting yarn. It is best to use a smooth yarn as it will be pulled out at a later stage. Finish the front and remove from the machine. Hold it the right way up, and with the face side towards the machine. Fold it back along the line marked with the contrast yarn. Bring the needles required for the width of the pocket to the knitting position. Pick the stitches from the centre of the marked row onto the needles. Knit the pocket, picking up a stitch from the body onto the edge needles every row.

Two edges may be cast off together to save having to stitch them together. For example, knit the back of a cardigan, shaping the shoulders by holding. Finish on waste yarn. Knit the left front, shaping the shoulders by holding. Pick the stitches of the left back shoulder onto the needles. Cast off. Repeat for the right side. Alternatively, knit the sleeve sideways, starting with the waste yarn and shaping by holding. Pick up the bottom edge onto the needles. Cast off. This gives a raised seam on the outside.

Figure 94 shows a jacket which was constructed entirely on the machine using some of the methods described, and which has no seams at all.

Cut and sew

There are two types of cut and sew knitwear. Fabric may be knitted in lengths, on the full width of the machine, and then cut and made up from paper patterns. The width of fabric, depending on the yarn and the stitch, will vary from 60 to 88cm (24 to 35 inches). Bottom edges may be hemmed, or ribs may be attached. The second method is to knit body blanks. A body blank is a rectangle whose dimensions correspond exactly to the overall height and width of the body shape required and which has a knitted hem or rib at the bottom. Neck, armhole and shoulder shaping must be cut out before making up.

In either case cut edges must be finished off to prevent unravelling. Modern automatic sewing machines will do overlocking, or reverse feed stitch for this purpose. Basic zigzag is adequate for most fabrics, and even a straight stitch will hold some. Oversewing by hand is suitable for small jobs. Regardless of how the edges are finished, hand sew the seams for the best finish.

A stable fabric is required for fabric lengths in order to cut an accurate pattern.

Weave fabrics are therefore the most suitable, and they have the added advantage that they do not unravel easily. Slip stitch fabrics are also relatively stable, but they require secure edge finishing. The advantage of cut and sew is that it saves knitting time and the time required to work out a pattern. Tailored garments may be made from fabric lengths, especially weave fabrics, or fabrics which have had an iron-on interlining applied to the back. New design ideas may be worked out with body blanks and cut and sew collars etc., so that they can be fitted before final cutting. This is especially useful since making paper toiles is of no use in knitwear because of the lack of stretch in the paper. Cut and sew may also be used to correct or re-use knitting which has not come out according to pattern.

Figure 94 Jacket without seams

Common Problems

Casting on

PROBLEM	CAUSE	REMEDY
carriage jams	carriage not properly on track	remove and replace as described on page 36
	cast on too tight	remove carriage and repeat more loosely
	yarn too tight	check that ball is wound loosely enough and check tensioner and yarn guides for tangling or knots
needles do not move	holding cam control on hold	slide carriage back across needles, re-set control, and repeat first row
all stitches dropped	yarn not fully in feeder	correct mistake and start again
	yarn in feeder 2	correct mistake and start again
	sinker plate not right in	correct mistake and start again
stitches dropped at beginning of row	yarn too loose	start again, adjust tensioner, and take up slack at beginning of row by hand
stitches dropped in middle of row	sinker plate not right in	loosen thumb screws, push plate in, and tighten
	yarn tangled in sinker brushes	clean brushes and start again
	cast on too loose	cast on more tightly
stitches tuck	cast on too tight or stitch tension too low	knit down by hand or start again and correct mistake
stitches not knitting	cast on too loose or controls not set to plain knitting	start again and correct mistake
stitches knit under cord in open cast on	cord not tight enough	pull cord tighter and continue, or start again
open cast on unravels when weights are added	cord removed too soon, or stitch tension too loose, or weights hung too low	start again and correct mistake

Plain knitting

The carriage may jam in the middle of a row. Follow the instructions given on page 36. A small knot or bump in the yarn is sometimes the cause of jamming, in which case a gentle tap on the carriage may get it going again. Only tap it very gently, or serious damage to the needle bed will result.

PROBLEM	CAUSE	REMEDY
all stitches drop off	no yarn in feeder, or yarn broken, or yarn end reached	replace knitting on needles; to avoid repetition watch out for yarn end approaching or tie beginning of new ball to tail of ball knitting
	yarn not properly in feeder	replace knitting on needles and thread yarn correctly
single stitch repeatedly dropped	needle bent	replace needle
stitches dropped at beginning of row	yarn take up spring not operating correctly	check that yarn is threaded correctly and that spring is not caught up; adjust tensioner; with heavy or textured yarn take up slack by hand at beginning of row
carriage stiff and occasional stitches dropped	yarn tangled in sinker wheels	remove carriage from needle bed and clean
all stitches tucking	stitch tension too low or yarn too tight	adjust tension and check free running of yarn
single stitch repeatedly tucking	needle latch bent	replace needle
stitches tucking at beginning of row	knitting too fast at end of row	unravel one row and continue
loops of yarn at edge or yarn tangling on sinker wheels	yarn take up spring not operating correctly or carriage taken too far and too fast on previous row	check threading of tensioner and that spring is not caught up; use a smoother knitting action as described on page 36.
stitches caught up on sinker pins	loose or irregular yarn tension	for a single stitch, poke crochet hook down behind stitches and lift yarn off pin; for several stitches pull knitting away from needles and up over pins without dropping stitches
yarn constantly breaking	weak or brittle yarn	rewind and re-wax yarn

Pattern knitting

PROBLEM	CAUSE	REMEDY
areas of plain instead of pattern at edge on Knitmaster/Studio	pattern row not cleared when knitting narrow pieces	take carriage right past pattern centre every row
areas of plain instead of pattern all across on Knitmaster/Studio	yarn tangled in pattern drum	remove carriage from bed and clean drums
card catching or tearing	card clipped wrong way	place bottom edge in front of top edge when clipping card
mistake in punch card	pattern punched incorrectly	punch new holes or place cellophane tape over holes
	holes not centred correctly	re-punch holes
stitch dropped at beginning of row	pattern stitch at beginning of row	bring first needle to forward position every row
tucks dropped	stitch tension too loose	change to lower tension
stitches knitting instead of tucking	weights too heavy	remove weights
edge stitch dropped in transfer lace	pattern stitch at edge	return edge needle to knitting position before transferring stitches
inlay yarn not weaving in	sinker plate not right in	unscrew, push in, and tighten
	weaving brushes not correctly fitted on Knitmaster	adjust
	weaving yarn tension not correct	adjust
	selector knob on 'N' on Brother lever model	change to 'T'

Picking up dropped stitches

A large dropped stitch may be picked back up by inserting the transfer tool and transferring the stitch back onto the needle. It is impossible to insert the transfer tool into a small dropped stitch. Some machines are equipped with a tool which has a conventional crochet hook at one end and a point at the other. Small stitches may be picked up with the pointed end. However it is easier to pick up the stitch below the one that was dropped.

Place it onto the empty needle. Bring the needle forward so that the stitch is behind the latch. Place the yarn of the dropped stitch in the hook, and knit a stitch back up (fig. 95). Use this method when the dropped stitch has laddered down a row or two.

For a longer ladder insert the latch hook into the first whole stitch from behind, i.e. the face side, and knit the necessary rows up to the needle. This is the same as shown in figure 67, but from the other side of the fabric to avoid making purl stitches.

If the knitting drops off the needles completely, pick up onto the needles with the transfer tool in the same way. Start at one end and pick up a stitch from each wale onto a needle. Do not worry which row the stitch is from. When all the needles have a stitch on, unpick several rows until a complete row is reached.

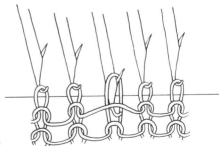

Figure 95

Unravelling on the machine

It is usually quickest, when a mistake has been made, to unravel down to below the mistake and re-knit. Push all the needles as far back as they will go behind the sinker gate, so that all stitches are held tight in the hooks of the needles. Starting on the same side as the carriage, pull the yarn tightly and exactly vertical above the first needle. The stitch will unpick and automatically transfer the stitch below up onto the needle. If it does not unpick immediately jerk the yarn slightly away from you. Unpick the whole row in this way. Push the needles back again before unpicking the next row. Count the number of rows unpicked so you will know where to re-commence pattern. If a knit tracer is being used, roll it back the appropriate number of rows.

If a punch card is being used, roll it back the appropriate number of rows. Set the card feed to hold. Disconnect the carriage from the pattern card. Set the carriage to knit slip. Pass the carriage across the knitting once or twice. The needles will not move. The correct pattern row has now been fed in. Connect the carriage to the pattern card, set the carriage to the required stitch, release the card, and continue knitting.

Replacing a needle

Needles are replaced in the same way on all machines. They are held in place by a strip of metal with a sponge cushion which fits in a tunnel under the front of the needle bed. The strip has white plastic tips. Push one end of the strip with the handle of the latch hook until the opposite end extends far enough to get a grip on it. Pull it out until the other end of it has cleared the needle to be replaced. Bring the needle to the forward position and tip it up at the back until the end clears the needle bed. Pull it out backwards at an angle. Repeat this in reverse to fit the new needle. Push the needle retaining strip back in.

Correcting mistakes off the machine

Ladders discovered after the knitting has been removed from the machine should be knitted up with the latch hook from the face side. Leave the latch hook in the last stitch knitted. Thread a blunt knitwear sewing needle with a length of the knitting yarn. Starting at the back, follow the course of the stitches in the row above the stitch in the latch hook. When this stitch is reached, knit it in. Finish on the reverse side. This mend is completely invisible when done correctly.

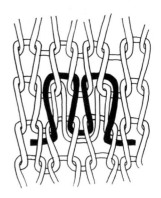

Figure 96

Holes caused by breaks in the yarn may be invisibly mended in a similar way. Start several stitches from the hole. Follow the stitches with the yarn threaded in the sewing needle. When the hole is reached, make stitches across it as in grafting. Follow several stitches past the hole to secure. Odd stitches knitted in the wrong colour in fairisle patterns may be corrected by sewing over in the correct colour by the same method (fig. 96).

Tightening ribs

Ribs which are too loose may be tightened up by steaming. Lay the knitting on the steam table. Pull it lengthways to close the ribs as much as possible. Pin the bottom of the rib to the table, using lots of pins close together, and gathering as you go. Make sure the edge is in a straight line. Gather the other end of the knitting in the hand, and pull to lengthen the rib. Still stretching the rib, place the wet cloth over and steam.

Correcting mistakes in size and shape

Knitted pieces coming out too large or too small all over are almost certainly caused by bad measurement of the tension swatch. A wrong shape is most likely caused by a mistake in working out the pattern. Small discrepancies may be corrected by steaming to the correct shape. The steaming may have to be repeated before the knitting retains its correct shape and size. It is easier to shrink away extra room in steaming than to stretch to a larger size. Small shapes may be made to fit by making extra large button bands etc. Large shapes may be cut and made up by the cut and saw method. If you have no means of finishing off cut edges, cut only edges which are to be finished with a double band, e.g. neck and front edges. If a piece has to be unpicked and re-knitted, wind the yarn into a skein, and hold it over a steaming kettle to lose the kinks before re-using.

Not Just Fashions

The knitting machine is capable of making a much wider range of things than just knitwear. By imaginative choice of yarns and techniques, fabrics suitable for many purposes may be made. Here are some suggestions of things to make, and points to bear in mind.

Fashion accessories

For jewellery, brooches, bracelets, etc., use knitted cord stitched into shapes, various three-dimensional techniques, and metallic yarns. For belts, bags and shoe uppers with a macramé look, use string knitted in lace or weave. Spaced needles and several waxings may be necessary before the string will knit smoothly.

Furnishings

Any attractive fabric is suitable for cushion covers if it is lined or backed. For upholstery, a hard-wearing opaque fabric with limited stretch is required. How hard-wearing it is will mainly depend on the choice of yarn. Opacity may be achieved by felting wool after knitting. Wash the fabric in hot water and rub vigorously. Or use a bulky, textured yarn either to knit with or as an inlay yarn. Knit on a tight tension.

The main problem with curtaining is to make a fabric which will not drop over an extended period. Use weaving or slip stitch fabrics hung sideways for maximum stability. With a sewing machine, stitch vertical parallel lines every few centimetres (inches) on any knitted fabric, hung lengthways, to increase stability.

For flat rugs, weave rug or carpet yarn with a finer yarn knitting. There are several ways of making pile rugs. Knit loops row by row as already des-

Figure 97 Curtain in natural coloured cotton and wool bouclé

Figure 98 Wallcovering fabric in natural coloured wool and cotton

Figure 99 Pair of space dividers of machine knitting and knotting

Figure 100 Knitted landscape by Ginny Hubble

cribed for a knitted in fringe. Knit a weaving pattern with long floats and cut through floats. Knit fringes, and then weave them into a backing fabric. Make a fabric with sections of needles out of knitting. Sew the edge of each solid section to its neighbour, so forming the floats into loops.

Many techniques are suitable for making bedspreads, but particularly appropriate is a fabric which is both light in weight and bulky. Ripple stitch using slip stitch on hold is one way of obtaining this. Use lace stitch for lampshades, and shape them by darting. Many techniques are suitable for table

mats, but choose cotton as the fibre most resistant to heat and constant washing. Use partial patterning, multi-coloured inlay, intarsia etc. for knitted pictures and wall-hangings. Make stuffed toys, and use darting for the ears, nose and other three-dimensional details. For seating, knit three-dimensional forms, and stuff them with foam.

Rigid three-dimensional forms, such as bowls and baskets, may be set with a sugar solution as follows. Knit a circle in cotton yarn in any stitch. Mix two parts sugar with one part water in a saucepan. Heat almost to the point of turning brown. Soak the

Figure 101 Knitted tapestry

cotton circle in the solution. Stretch over a basin for a mould and allow to dry. It will set in the form of the mould used, and will be quite rigid and not at all sticky. When it eventually gets grubby, boil out the old solution and re-set.

A useful way to finish anything which is going to be difficult or impossible to wash is to treat it with a silicone aerosol spray. This is designed primarily as a water proofing treatment, but it also prevents staining and dust and grime becoming embedded in the fibres. It does not detract in any way from the natural appearance of the fabric.

Figure 102 Knitted chair by Betty Barnden

Weight Conversion Table

Ounces to grams calculated to the nearest whole gram.

1oz = 28.35gms

OZ	GMS	OZ	GMS
1	28	9	255
2	57	10	283
3	85	11	312
4	113	12	340
5	142	13	369
6	170	14	397
7	198	15	425
8	227	16	454

Glossary

Bird's eye	spotted pattern of alternate plain and pattern stitches
Butt	see 'needle butt'
Double rib	imitation rib made by knitting a hem with needles out
Face side	side of knitting facing machine during knitting
Holding cam	control which prevents needles brought right forward from moving when carriage is passed across them
Inlay yarn	non-knitting yarn in weave or inlay knitting
Knit tracer	device for translating drawn pattern into shaping instructions
Latch	movable part of needle which opens and closes hook
Latch hook	tool similar to knitting needle but fitted with a plastic handle
Needle butt	part of needle which projects above needle bed
Needle out	type of knitting where some needles are left in the non-knitting position and do not pick up stitches
Purl stitch	stitch made from reverse side of knitting either by latch hook or ribbing attachment
Reverse side	side of knitting facing knitter during knitting
Rib	knitting which has both wales of plain and wales of purl stitches
Short row	technique for changing direction of knitting before the end of a row
Sinker brush	brush on underneath of sinker plate which holds knitting against sinker pins when needles move
Sinker gate	row of pins along front of needle bed
Sinker pin	one of the pins making up the sinker gate
Sinker plate	front detachable part of carriage which carries the yarn feed, sinker brushes and wheels, and weaving brushes
Sinker wheel	wheel on underneath of sinker plate which holds knitting against sinker pins when needles move
Tension	knitting tension is dependent on the size of stitch selected – the higher the stitch size the looser the knitting
Tensioner	system of springs and eyes set on rod at back of needle bed to ensure that yarn is fed to needles at the correct tension

Tracer	see 'knit tracer'
Wale	vertical column of stitches
Waste knitting	temporary knitting of contrasting colour which is unravelled either at a later stage of knitting or during making up
Waste yarn	yarn used for waste knitting
Yarn feed	point on sinker plate where yarn is fed to needles

Bibliography

Introduction
Henson's History of the Framework Knitters (1831), David & Charles
Wignall, H., *Knitting*, Pitman

Which machine?
Weaver, Mary, *Passap Duomatic*, Weaver Knits
Weaver, Mary, *The Ribbing Attachment, part 1*, Weaver Knits

Yarns
Miller, Edward, *Textiles: Properties and Behaviour*, Batsford
Mark, Herman F. (Ed.), *Giant Molecules*, Time-Life International
Maille, Anne, *Tie and Dye Made Easy*, Mills & Boon

Creating Fabrics
Norbury, James, *Traditional Knitting Patterns*, Dover
Thompson, Gladys, *Guernsey and Jersey Patterns*, Batsford
Abbey, Barbara, *The Complete Book of Knitting*, Thames & Hudson
Jones Knitting Patterns, Jones Sewing Machine Co Ltd
Punch Card Pattern, Jones Sewing Machine Co Ltd
Cassette Knitting Patterns, Jones Sewing Machine Co Ltd
Pattern Library for Punchcard Knitters, Knitmaster Ltd

Not Just Fashions
Cone, F.G., *Knit-Art*, Van Nostrand Reinhold
Walker Phillips, Mary, *Creative Knitting*, Van Nostrand Reinhold

List of Suppliers

Machine Manufacturers

UK

Brother
Jones Sewing Machine Co Ltd
J and B House
869 High Road, Finchley
London N12 82W
Tel. 01-446 3231

Knitmaster Ltd
30–40 Elcho Street
London SW11 4AX
Tel. 01-228 9303

Passap Ltd
128–129 High Street
Bordesley
Birmingham 12
Tel. 021 772 5600

The Singer Co Ltd
255 High Street
Guildford
Surrey GU1 3DH
Tel. 0483 71144

Toyota
Aisin (UK) Ltd
Unit 32 Rich Industrial Estate
Crayford Road
Crayford
Kent
Tel. 0332 522256/7

USA

Brother
Brother International
900 Lunt Avenue
Elk Grove Village, Illinois 60007
Tel. (800) 323–0592

Passap Knitting Machines
A C Weber & Co Inc
505 Washington Avenue
Carlstadt, NY 07072

The Singer Company
321 First Street
Elizabeth, NJ 07207

The Singer Sewing Company
30 Rockefeller Plaza
New York, NY 10020

Studio
Studio Yarn Farms Inc (US distributor)
10024 14th Avenue SW
Seattle, Washington 98146
Tel. (206) 763–1310

Toyota
Newton Knits (US distributor)
9836 Garden Grove Boulevard
Garden Grove, California 92644
Tel. (714) 530–6551

Knitting Machine Dealers Association
222–15 Braddock Avenue
Queens Village, New York 11428
Tel. (212) 776–3018
For information on all knitting
machines available in
the USA

Yarn Suppliers
UK

Camden Weavers
16 Lower High St
Chipping Camden, Glos.

Fancy weaving yarns, some suitable for knitting.

Hilary Chetwynd
Kipping Cottage
Cheriton
Alresford, Hants

Pure silk yarns.

The Direct Wool Group
PO Box 46
Bradford BD1 2AN

Hand knitting yarns in balls.

R.S. Duncan & Co
Falcon Mills
Bartle Lane
Bradford BD7 4QJ

Hand knitting yarns in balls, machine knitting accessories, orders by return

Foster Textile Sales
Market Street West
Preston.

Fine wool and courtelle on cones.

Wm. Hall & Co Ltd
Cheadle Hulme
Cheshire

Plain and fancy cottons, rayon and chenille, on tubes.

Hayfield Textiles Ltd
Hayfield Mills
Glusburn, Keighley

Synthetics specially designed for domestic knitting machines.

Holmefirth Wools
Briggate
Windhill
Shipley BD18 2BS

Hand knitting yarns in balls and on cones, orders by return.

Holywell Textile Mills Ltd
Holywell CH8 7NU
North Wales

Welsh wool in oil on cones, including Jacob's Sheep's wool in natural colours.

T.M. Hunter Ltd
Sutherland Wool Mills
Brora KW9 6NA
Scotland

Best quality Scottish wools in hanks, minimum order 10 lbs.

Jamieson & Smith Ltd
90 North Road
Lerwick ZE1 0PQ
Shetland Isles

Traditional Shetland wools in hanks and on cones.

Knitwell Wools Ltd
Boromill
116 Sunbridge Road
Bradford BD1 2NF

Hand knitting yarns in balls and some on cones.

St Johns Knitting Wool Co
PO Box 55
39 Well Street
Bradford BD1 5NG

Hand knitting yarn in hanks and on cones, orders by return.

Texere Yarns
9 Peckover Street
Bradford BD1 5BD

Wide range of fancy weaving yarns mainly on cones, some suitable for knitting; good value.

J.L. Walton & Son
26 Newarke Street
Leicester LE1 5SL

Synthetic/natural knitwear yarns, minimum order 25lbs; good value.

Wool Fashion Bureau Ltd
PO Box 16
Wakefield WF2 9BR

Hand knitting yarns in balls, orders by return.

USA

Austral Enterprises
POB 70190
Seattle, Washington 98107

Crêpe, bouclé, and Welsh four-ply wools; catalog and yarn cards; mail order available.

Bare Hill Studios
(Reba Maisel)
East Bare Hill Road
Harvard, Massachusetts
01451

Mill ends; sample yarns and mail order available.

Colonial Woolen Mills Inc
6501 Berberton Avenue
Cleveland, Ohio 44102

100-percent virgin Shetland, acrylics, wool blends; catalog and yarn samples; minimum mail order.

Fibre Yarn Company Inc
840 Sixth Avenue
New York, New York 10001

Wide assortment of yarns; minimum quantity policy; mail order available.

House of Yarns and Crafts
POB 403
Route 1, Lafayette Road
Seabrook, New Hampshire
03874

Metallic yarns, mohair-like acrylics, imported homespuns; catalog and yarn sample cards; mail order available.

Lilly Mills Company
POB 88
Shelby, North Carolina
28150

Cottons, linens, synthetics; catalog and yarn sample cards; mail order available.

Mary Maxim Inc
2001 Holland Avenue
Port Huron, Michigan
48060

Wools, mohairs, angora; catalog; mail order available.

Meg Swansen
Trumansburg, New York
14886

Icelandic unspun wool, unbleached natural sheepswool Shetland wool; yarn sample card; mail order available.

Naturalcraft
2199 Bancroft Way
Berkeley, California 94704

Silk, synthetic silk, cashmere, chenille; catalog; mail order available.

The Niddy Noddy
416 Albany Post Road
Croton-on-Hudson,
New York 10520

Yarns, knitting machines; catalog; mail order available.

Village Weaving Center
434 Sixth Avenue
New York, New York
10011

Hand knitting yarns on cones and in skeins; wools including Shetlands; wool blends; minimum mail order 1 oz per color.

List of Brand Name Equivalents in Various Countries

Machines are sold under different brand names in different countries. The table shows the UK brand names which are used throughout the book, with, below each, the brand names under which each is sold in other countries.

United Kingdom	Knitmaster	Singer Memomatic	Brother	Toyota
Japan	Silver	Juki	Brother	Toyota
United States	Studio	Juki	Brother	Toyota
Europe	Empisal	Juki/Erka	—	Toyota
Australia	Singer Memomatic	—	Empisal Knitmaster	—
New Zealand	Singer Memomatic	—	Empisal Knitmaster	Toyota
South Africa	—	—	Empisal Knitmaster	Singer Memomatic
South America	Singer Memomatic	—	—	Toyota
East Africa	Singer Memomatic	—	Brother	—

Index

Numbers in bold type refer to illustrations.